30 Step Off!

the hardest thirty days of your life

by Justin Lookadoo

Extreme for Jesus Brand Manager, Hayley Morgan.
Cover Design, Toby Taylor.
Editor, Kate Etue.
Packaging, Barbara West.
Page Design, Matt Lehman.

Scripture quotations are from the New King James Version of the Bible © 1982 by Thomas Nelson Publishers.

Library of Congress Cataloging-in-Publication Data

Lookadoo, Justin.
        Step off: the hardest 30 days of your life / by Justin Lookadoo.
                p. cm.
                ISBN 0-7852-4604-5
                1. Christian teenagers—Religious life. I. Title.

BV4531.3 L66 2001

248.8'3—dc21

00-054816

Printed in the United States of America
1 2 3 4 5 6 -- 06 05 04 03 02 01

Step Off!

table of contents

····❖ Intro

Here's the deal. You are about to do things you never thought you could. You are not going to live on the edge—that's for wimps. You are going to walk up to the edge and step off. You will push yourself further than you ever thought possible. The ride of your life has just begun, and there's no stopping in the middle.

You can go it alone, but I don't suggest it. Grab a bud or two or five and go through this together. You are going to need the encouragement. But hey, if you are set on going solo...rage on!

These are going to be the hardest 30 days of your life. Step Off is set up for you to do 5 out of 7 days. You are going to need a couple of days a week to catch your breath. Take the time. Chill. Read. Whatever. Just pace yourself so you will make it.

Get ready to have your world twisted, your mind blown, and your spirit filled. Get up and STEP OFF.

STEP OFF is dedicated to those who knew I deserved death, but let me live....my parents. Frank and Mary Lookadoo (see that is our real name). They taught me that there is nothing I can not do. Because of them I learned to STEP OFF and live life to the fullest. A special thanks to Dad. You taught me how to be a man. You never sat me down and gave me a lesson. You taught me by living your life as the man I want to be. And to Mom. In an airport in Lubbock, Texas, you told me to do something that has become my life goal...."Live With No Regrets". I love you. Thanks.

Calendar

M	T	W	T	F
Road Map	$100 Commitment	Lifestyle	Got Symbols?	Media Fast
Media Fast Again	Get In or Get Out	Prayer	Bible Surfing	1/2 Day Getaway
Christian Ghetto	Friend-ventory	Give Away What???	Did You Do It?	Learning to Surf
Food for Sex or Sex-Free	Sex Symbol	Character Quiz	Attitude	Media Fast
Salty Fun	Au Natural	Horoscope	Love-Fest	333
Attitude Check	You're Dead	Funky Feet	Clean Fee	Last Day... First Day

day1

**Let's start with a test.
Ready?** Here goes.
What is this?

TEXAS

If you said anything other than a map, then
we need to sit down and talk. **Yes, it's a
map.** Second question. What do you get
from a map? Directions, very good. So you
use a map to get directions to go somewhere.
OK, last question. Using this map, give me
directions to Canada.
Write them down here:

Answer that one. You can't? Why not? Oh,
because Canada is not there.
Kind of hard to get directions to Canada
using a Texas map, eh?

THE WORD

That is exactly what could be happening
with you and this Bible study.

Check it out. I Corinthians 2:14. **You**
have to get your Bible and look it up. It's
a Bible study. It's in the New Testament.
Don't just keep reading. Look it up 'cuz I
am not going to write it down for you.
I'll wait...

Read it.

If you were going to guess what that verse has to do with the map, what would you say?
C'mon take a guess. **Write it down.**

The Map Symbolizing

God's Word

If you didn't guess, go back and write something down. Even if it doesn't make sense, that's groovy too.
Just take a guess.

OK, HERE'S THE DEAL. If your destination is not heaven, then you are getting directions for a trip that you are not on. You are getting info for a life that you are not living. **Let's break it down a little more.** You can go to church, pray, do a Bible study thing, but if you have not given Jesus control of your life, **it really won't make any difference.** Sure, you will get some directions on how to live a "good" life, but it won't really click for you. Like if you're using a Texas map to get to Canada. Sure you will get some general directions on how to go north, but, in the big picture, it won't help much.

LIFE LINK!

For the wages of sin is death, but the gift of God is eternal life in Christ Jesus our Lord.
(Romans 6:23)

. . . .

Learn it. Memorize it. Get a box of index cards. Write this verse on one of them. Put it somewhere so you can see it bunches. **Get it in your head to stay.** You will have a LIFE LINK! verse almost every day. Write them each on a different card. Keep them with you so you can look at them and learn them.

STEP OFF.

Heaven or hell.

It's your choice. God does not send anyone to hell.
They choose hell. For the wages of sin is death. We
earn death--hell. But the God thing is that He gives
us a gift. Life--Heaven. It's your choice.

All we have to do is:

❶ Believe that Jesus is the Son of God; He died for our sins and rose from the dead.
❷ Give Jesus control of our life, our decisions, everything.

Have you ever done that? Have you ever made the decision to let Jesus control your life?

If you have, write down what happened.
What were you doing? Where were you?
Who was there? What was going on around you?

I was at a Junior high summer camp, I discovered my need for a Savior and I got Babtized

If you haven't or are not sure, let's make it easy.

❶ We have all screwed up. We all sin. Everyone.
❷ But Jesus died for us. He was the sacrifice for our mess-ups.
❸ If we give Jesus control of our life...we're in!

day 1
{continued}

Easy. **Jesus wants you to be His.**
If you want to give your life to Him and be saved, then
read the following prayer. Read it and say it to God.
Prayer just means a conversation between you and
God. **So, talk to God.**

**"God, I know that I mess up. I am a sinner. I
believe your Son, Jesus, died for my sin, and He
rose from the dead. I give you control of my life.
Take me just like I am, and make me who you want
me to be. Thank you for saving me. Amen."**

Rock on!! If you said that and meant it, **everything in your past is GONE.**
All of those bad things are forgotten by God. Yeah, there may still be some consequences lurking around, but God has totally forgiven you.

**If you just asked Jesus to rule your life, then write down
today's date.For Christians, this is kind of like a new birth-
day. You have become a child of God.**

Now, call your youth group leader or another Christian adult and tell that person
what just happened.
The next time you talk to someone in your youth group, tell them what happened.
This is so cool.
**YOU HAVE JUST STEPPED OFF THE EDGE INTO THE
REAL RUSH OF LIVING LIFE TO THE FULLEST.**

Ya gotta know something. It is OK not to know what's next. When I gave my life to Jesus, I didn't have a clue what all was happening. I was a sinner. Jesus loved me and wanted to save me. I said, "OK." That's all I knew to do. So don't weird out if you're a little lost. You will learn and grow with time.

CONGRATS! YOU ARE A CHILD OF THE KING.

/!\ **CAUTION:** If you have not made the decision to turn your life over to Jesus and you are not going to-- STOP NOW. This is the most important decision you will ever make in your life. It is also the foundation for knowing God and doing STEP OFF. Remember, if you have not given God control, you'll be getting directions for a journey you are not on. So either get in the journey or get out of the study.

GET READY TO STEP OFF.
Did You Do It? _____Yes_____
make a commitment? _____Yes_____

DAY2 ★★★

What if when you got this book I handed you a **$100** bill? Would you take it? (I know. Duh! But work with me for a second.) How much would it be worth? Hundred bucks. Cool. What if I rubbed it under my armpits? Would you take it? Sure! Cuz how much is it worth now? Same. What if I wadded it up into a little ball, spit on it, threw it on the ground, and stepped on it? Now how much is it worth? Hundred smackeroos. Nothing we did changed the value. It was still worth the same. **And free money is good money.**

THE WORD

There are a lot of teens that are Christians, **but feel so far away from God.** Your life is so wacked out by the way you are living. You are out in the scene, boozin' or dopin' it up. Or you're a Christian and you're having sex with your boyfriend or girlfriend. Or the things that come out of your mouth are just total yuckness. **No Jesus there.** You feel like you have gotten so far away from God that He doesn't want to have anything to do with you. You feel worthless and when someone says God loves you, you say things like, **"But you don't know what I've done."**

6

DAY 2
continued

Check out what the Word says about you: Luke 15:11-32.

Don't miss the bus here. This isn't just some cool story that you learned when you were a little kid.

This is about you. Now. Today.

You may have run off from your Father (God). You did your own thing. You partied and sexed it up. You failed out of school. You got an abortion, or whatever your baggage is that is keepin' you down. You've been living like you aren't even part of God's family. Well, it's time to come home.

God--Dad--is waiting on you. He wants you to come back.

You are the son in the story. God is the Father. Just like the father, God wants to hug you and throw a party because you are back. And that blah-blah excuse of, "If he knew what I have done, He wouldn't want me back," doesn't cut it. He does know, and He does want you!!

You are the $100 bill. God sees you as His valuable child. You may have messed up big time. **You are still $100.** You may have crumbled up, stomped on, and totally trashed your life. But you are still worth the same today as you were the first day you gave your life to God.

LIFE LINK!

If we confess our sins, He is faithful and just to forgive us our sins and to cleanse us from all unrighteousness.
(I John 1:9)

Again, take out a card and write the verse down. Learn it. Test others in your crew. Push each other to get these verses in your life.

DAY 2 continued

STEP OFF.
DO-OVER!!!!

If you have gone off and done your own thing and have not really worried about where Jesus was in your life, then right now is for you. **DO-OVER!!!** That's what is so cool about God. He's OK with do-overs. He wants you to come back to Him. **He is still there.** He's waiting on you to make a move.

> What are some things that you've been into that you know are so not God? **Scribe it! Don't just keep reading. This is for you and God. (You don't have to show it to anyone else.)**

_____
_____
_____
_____

What are some actions, thoughts, baggage you have that you want to get rid of? **(drugs, jealousy, sex, lying, laziness, etc.)**

_____
_____
_____
_____

DO-OVER RULES:

1. Tell God that you are **sorry** that you have run away from Him and ignored Him.

2. Tell God **thank you** for taking you back and letting you start over.

3. Tell your group about it. Tell them that you made a commitment to **follow** Christ full-on.

Pray something like this:

"Father, I know I ran away from you. I'm sorry. Forgive me for (you have to fill in the blank). I am back. I know you love me. Thanks for welcoming me back. Help me get stronger so I won't run away again."

If you have stayed with the Father and your relationship with God is solid and getting stronger, then write a short prayer right now about two things.

1. THANK HIM FOR KEEPING YOU CLOSE.
2. PRAY THAT EVERYONE IN THE GROUP WILL STAY SOLID.

_____

_____

_____

God loves you no matter what you've done.
He wants you to ask for a do-over.
Get back to God and STEP OFF.

Jorge **was a teenager living in** the body of a hulk of a man. His short sixteen years had experienced a lot. The scars on his side and back told chilling tales of knife fights and drive-bys.

I met Jorge when he was **locked up** in a juvenile detention facility for gang-related crimes. **He wanted to change.** He knew he had to change.

After Jorge left lockup we kept in touch. He was all about starting fresh. But it wasn't long before his old set started coming around. They kept up the **pressure.** Not only was Jorge the baddest in the clique, but he was OG. **He was the last living original gangsta of their set.**

The more Jorge tried to pull away, the more they pressured him. Finally, Jorge couldn't take the pressure.
He made his choice.

I saw Jorge for the last time. As we said good-bye, this 6'2, 225 lb. rock cried. He broke down. We prayed together, and he told me that he would not live to be twenty-one. And he didn't.

THE WORD

What happened? Check it out: **Matthew 9:14-17**

Jorge wanted to change. But like it says in the Word, he was putting new wine in an old wineskin. It didn't work. Jorge wanted to live differently. He wanted to change his life. But he tried to put new life into an old lifestyle. The new life was lost.

day
03

LIFE LINK!

Therefore, if anyone is in Christ, he is a new creation; old things have passed away; behold, all things have become new.

(2 Corinthians 5:17)

YEP. YOU KNOW WHAT TO DO. LEARN IT.

STEP OFF

New life must be put into a new lifestyle. Some of us haven't bought into this yet. You are a Christian. **You have given your life to God, but you haven't changed your lifestyle.** You are trying to put new wine in your old wineskin. You haven't changed what you do. You haven't changed who you hang out with, the jokes you tell. Anything that does not jive with what God wants is old wineskin.

day 03

↙

ARE THERE SOME OLD WINESKINS IN YOUR LIFE?

Old habits, gossip, wearing certain clothes, sex, drugs, gangs. For you, what are your old wineskins?

Old habits

What do you need to do to change your lifestyle?
What is the first thing that you are going to do?
BE SPECIFIC.

Stop being so
lazy

day
03

↙

When you get with your group, **give 'em the goods on what you need to change. Let them do the same.** Everyone brainstorm and get a plan on how to help each other be a success. Alone you will fail. With others you can do anything. If it is way too personal to share with the group, then get with your youth minister and talk through it.

GET GOING. CHANGE YOU.
CHANGE YOUR LIFE. STEP OFF.

The world would be a much cleaner place if we ate our own trash.

day⁴

I was driving through a small country town.
You know the kind with a gas station, post office, and one stop sign in the middle of town. I cruised up to the stop sign. No one was around. So I just kind of, almost, **but not really,** stopped.

I rolled on through the stop sign. With a quickness I saw flashing lights in my mirror. Yikes-o-rama! I pulled over and this big bellied, small-town sheriff walked up to the window and said, "Boy, you ran that stop sign." I said, "No I didn't. I practically stopped. No one was coming so I paused and went really slow through it. What's the difference?"

The sheriff stepped back and said, "What's the difference? What's the difference?" He jerked me out of the car, took his stick, and started beating me in the head! And then, in the middle of his pounding, he shouted, **"Do you want me to stop or just go real slow?** What's the difference?"

THE WORD

Wondering what the Word could have to do with that experience? Well, did I see the stop sign? Did it make me stop? Nope. Did a cop really beat me in the head? No. But you get my point. Does a stop sign ever make you stop? We see them every day. I have never had a stop sign jump off its pole into my car and slam on the brakes.

Then what do stop signs do? What are they? **A stop sign is a symbol.** It reminds us of what we are supposed to do.

16

Okay, let's get our story hooked up with the Scripture. Get out the Word and go to the first book of the Bible. Genesis 8:20-21 and 9:8-17. Check out what it says.

Let's put it in real world issues. It's like this. When we get our driver's license we enter into a covenant, a Bible word that means "make a deal". So we make a deal with the state saying we will obey the traffic laws. (It's like God making a deal with us that He won't do a mambo-killer flood again.) Then the state puts up stop signs as reminders of our deal to follow the laws (the rainbow thing).

God uses symbols to remind us of the deals we've made. Altars were used a lot in the Bible. They were actually just a bunch of rocks piled up. Everyone who walked by would remember and think about why they were there. Noah built altars. Moses, David, they all built altars to **remind them of something God had done, said, or promised.**

LIFE LINK!

Commit your works to the Lord, and your thoughts will be established.
Proverbs 16:3
When God makes a deal, it's done. **He keeps His Word.** He wants us to do the same.
You know the wassup! Get a card. Write the verse. Learn it.

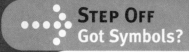

God even told people to have symbols. This isn't some freaky weird thing. **Check it.** Here's another short Scripture before we walk through making our own symbols. **Get your Word back out and look up Numbers 15:37-40**

See, the Father wants us to remember who He is and who we are. It's a lot easier to remember what's up if you have a reminder. So let's go through how to do altars and symbols. They are not just ol' time Bible stuff.

They're about today. **Your issues. Your life.**

LET'S TAKE A LOOK AT THE ISSUES.
FIRST, MAKE THE DEAL.
SECOND, GET THE SYMBOL.

The Deal: Commit that you will do what is asked in this Bible Study. All of it. You are going to be pushed way past what average Bible studies do. But we are not going for average.

We are stepping off over the edge into knowing God full-on. Write down what your deal is with God. What is your commitment with this Bible Study?

EXAMPLE: GOD, I WANT TO KNOW YOU. I COMMIT TO DOING THE STUFF IN THIS BIBLE STUDY, NO MATTER WHAT. I KNOW THAT I WILL SEE YOU IN NEW WAYS. I WILL NOT GIVE UP OR QUIT. HEY POSER! WRITE DOWN YOUR OWN DEAL WITH GOD. DON'T RIP ME OFF . . .

God, I commit to doing everything in this study. I pray you will give me strength & dedication. I want to know you more.

THE SYMBOL: Go get some rocks. Yes, rocks. Small, stackable rocks. Go get them! Right Now. Don't sit there. It's time to make an altar.

1   Write down your deal with God on a small piece of paper. Also, write down the LIFE LINK! verse on the paper. (Proverbs 16:3)

2   Find a place where you can stack your rocks. Bathroom counter. Dresser. TV stand. A place where you will see it every day. (Hint: also a place where you won't knock them over every day)

3   Put the paper down. Stack the rocks on top.

4   Pray again about your commitment. Tell God you're in. You commit to **STEP OFF.**

That's it. That's an altar. A symbol of your deal with God to do everything in STEP OFF. Even if it is hard. It's not a commitment with me, your friends, or your youth group leader. It's between you and God.

Every day when you see the altar think about your commitment and ask God to help you. When you get bummed out and you are ready to quit and bounce the group, go look at the altar. Read your commitment. Remember that you made a deal with the Creator of the Universe.

This symbol-making isn't a one-time-thing. Anytime God shows you something or gives you a promise or you just want a reminder of something, get a symbol.

Here are some examples of symbol-worthy things for me. I'll tell you that I am the trash jewelry king, so most of my symbols are trash jewelry.

Key ring. I have a necklace with a round key ring on it. The key ring is a symbol of God's best. I make plans that I know are good. But they get shot down because He doesn't want to give me good. He wants to give me His best.
>   Jeremiah 29:11--"For I know the thoughts that I think toward you, says the Lord, thoughts of peace and not of evil, to give you a future and a hope."

Rubber Bands. I wear rubber bands on my wrist to remind me to be careful what I look at, read, and do on the Internet.

> I Thessalonians 4:7--"For God did not call us to uncleanness, but in holiness."

Ring. A ring with a cross on it is a symbol of staying sexually pure, of not even putting myself in situations where I could fail.

> Ephesians 5:3--"But among you there must not be even a hint of sexual immorality, or of any kind of impurity, or of greed, because these are improper for God's holy people." (NIV)

Symbols will change what we do. Not because they're magic or anything like that, but because they totally change our focus. They are just like the stop signs. They don't make us do anything. They remind us of what we should do and who God wants us to be.

If you didn't make a commitment and build an altar to do the stuff in this book, please accept this "Get Out Invite." Tell your leader, "I'm out." You can get back in another group when you are ready. But if you are not going to commit to doing everything (which includes getting some rocks and making an altar) in STEP OFF then step out. You'll be in the way. So please accept this "Get Out Invite."

For the committed: look for ways to make symbols and STEP OFF.

Did You Do It?
make a symbol? _yes_

⊘day5

Zeta was incredible. We had gone to school together for several years. She was the package! **Fun. Exciting.** Eye candy to the Blizap! **Walking perfection!** She started dating Dusty. It didn't take long to see the change in Zeta.

I mean everyone saw the negativity growing in her. She stopped laughing. She never smiled. She wouldn't even look people in the eye. She just stared at the ground all the time in a downer funk.

Why the mega-change? Dusty. Her boyfriend of two years dogged her out every chance he got. He would do it in front of his friends and her friends. He would tell her how ugly and stupid she was and that if she ever left him she would never get another date because no one else could stand being around her. For two years that is all she heard. He had created a psycho-prison around Zeta that trapped her into believing the lies.

THE WORD

Hang with me now. This is not a story about hooking up with the right hottie. The deal is--if you hear something long enough you believe it. Truth becomes irrelevant.

Check it out. Grab the Word. The story is in Judges 16:1-22. Whoa. Don't just keep reading here. **Take out the Word and read the story.**

Did you see it? Did you see what happened?

Samson was this guy who was set apart by God since his birth. Samson had this strength thing going, and he knew God was with him. God was going to use Samson to help free all of his friends and relatives because the Philistines were keeping them down.

So what happened? Yeah, Samson knew

that he was set apart for God's work and that he was strong, but he was more interested in clowning around, using his gifts to get what he wanted and not totally give his life to God. He was forever hanging out with people and doing things that brought him down.

And remember, if you hear something long enough, you will buy into it. Samson met Delilah. She was a major babe.

Samson so wanted to be loved and accepted by her more than anything else. Every day she nagged him about his strength. Every day she would tell Samson that if he loved her he would tell her the secret.   He listened to the junk Delilah was telling him, and he bought into it. He broke.

Samson, this guy with insane physical strength, was totally destroyed because of who he listened to and what he allowed to grow in his mind.

[**WHAT DOES ALL THIS MEAN? IT AIN'T BRAIN SURGERY: "GARBAGE IN, GARBAGE OUT."**]

day5

ANSWER THIS:

What do you listen to most? What kind of music? Who is it?
Write it down.

Music, Frank Sinatra

What do you watch the most?

ESPN

What do you do the most? Video Games? Web surfing and dot.com-ing?

Video Games

Whatever you listen to and experience the most will shape what you believe and what you do. It's like this. If you absorb yourself in TV shows, it won't take long to decide that you must not be normal if you are not a neurotic, homosexual, work-a-holic, sex-addicted witch from a dysfunctional family. That's wacked! But remember, truth is irrelevant, and you will believe what you consistently hear.

LIFE LINK!

And do not be conformed to this world, but be **transformed** by the renewing of your mind, that you may prove what is that good and acceptable and perfect will of God.
(Romans 12:2)

Learn it! **Memorize this verse.**
Get another card and write this verse down.

STEP OFF

It's time to push life and STEP OFF.
How?

 21 Day Media Fast.

What does that mean? **No TV, no computer games, no surfin', and only music that talks about good stuff.** You know what we're talking about. If it talks about partying, romance, sex, drugs, or backin' any kind of thang up--it's out! Make it music that helps you focus on who God is (praise music, music that is all about God).

Hey, quit whining! It's only 21 days. Mark it on your calendar and count it down. This is important!!!

Why are we doing this? Our thoughts get so junked because of all the stuff we watch and listen to. It's time we take control of our mind and what goes in it.

Commit to this and you will be amazed at what happens. It will be hard, but it will be worth it.

So, cut out all the media stuff for the next **21 days.** If you are in the house and everyone is watching TV, go find something else to do. No, not video games. Go read. Hang out with your friends. Heaven forbid, talk to the parentals.

OK, time to make a plan.

First. Commit to a 21 Day Fast. Write down, "I commit to a 21 Day Media Fast." Then sign your name.

I commit to a 21 day media fast! ~~Joseph Borg~~

Now, when you are jonesing for that TV or dot.com fix, what are you gonna do? Write it down!

Play guitar

What are some other things you could do?

read, work out, etc

What is the verse that you will focus on? Write it down.
(For the clueless: it's Romans 12:2.)

Romans 12:2

Every time you want to chew on some media chunks, take out your verse--Romans 12:2. Read it and learn it.

What do you think will happen when you go on a 21 Day Media Fast? What will change, or what do you think you could get out of it? Guess! This isn't a test.

I will stop being so addicted to video games

Give it up! Ask God to help you commit to the 21 Day Media Fast. Ask Him to show you what He wants you to experience over the 21 days. Write a short prayer about it now.

Dear Lord, give me your strength and help me to stay committed

See you tomorrow!

Did you do it? _Yes_ No TV? _yes_

How's it going?

Has the stomach of your mind started rumbling from lack of media overload?

If you have already failed, don't give up. Commit to the 21 days. Get connected with the rest of your group. Help them and let them help you stay focused.

Isaiah 40:29 says, "He gives strength to the weary and increases the power of the weak" (NIV).

You can't stay strong, but God can. Let Him do it.

Now, if you're just a slacker and did not commit to the "media fast" for 21 days and you don't plan on doing it--**GET OUT!** Yes, that's right. Stop doing this journey and get out of the group. Listen, if you are not going to push life and step off into living with raging abandonment for Christ, then you are not going to benefit from this study and you will bring the group down.

So if you get out of the study then what do you do? Seek to know God. Pray that He will bring you to a point where you are ready to STEP OFF. Stay in touch with your youth group leaders and let them help you get ready so you can join the next group.

THE WORD

OK, back to those who are still with us.

Check this out: **Matthew 12:33-37.**

Look at the part about stuff "stored up" in you. How do you "store up" stuff inside you?

Studying, memorizing, learning, etc.

In what ways do things get into your mind and heart?

By Understanding them

How can you store up good stuff? _By studying it, memorizing it, learning, etc_

How can you store up bad stuff? _by allowing it to have a place in your life_

At the end there is a lot of weight put on our words. Why? Why is what we say so important? What do our words tell about us?

They tell how We feel. Sometimes they are the first thing People meeting us, see.

So how does any of this relate to the 65 Day Media Fast? (Ha, just checking to see if you were paying attention.) The 21 Day Media Fast—let's see.

Think about your last couple of days.

Have you wanted to veg-out with the TV, music, or Web?

Yes, mostly TV

What has been your biggest desire to get into?

_TV_

What did you do to fight the urge?

Read my Bible, homework, guitar

What is the Scripture that you focused on?

Romans 12:2 & Proverbs 13:3

This media fast, it's tough.

But hey, know that you are not the only one.

Call **two** compadres from your group.

See how they are doing and how their day went.

Ask them the ¿questions? you just answered.

✳ LIFE LINK!

And do not be conformed to this world, but be transformed by the renewing of your mind, that you may prove what is that good and acceptable and perfect will of God. (Romans 12:2)

Remember this from yesterday? If you haven't written it on a card yet, do it now. Try to say as much as possible without looking. Read it three times.
Each time try to get a little closer to knowing it.

STEP OFF

Write down all the cool things you can think of about God. It can be stuff in the Bible, things you've heard, or things that you have experienced with God. Write a list of those things.

God is merciful, God loves us, God is miraculous, God is Powerful, God is wise/all knowing.

That's called praising God. Telling Him who He is in our lives and what we love about Him. Telling Him who He is also reminds us **who we are and who we are not.**

Check out the verse again: **Romans 12:2.**

Read it. Turn it into a prayer about your 21 Day Media Fast. Write the prayer.

Lord, Help me not to be conformed by the world, but help me to be transformed by the renewing of my mind in this fast.

If you want, make a symbol to remind you of the 21 days. My symbol was simple. It was a note card taped to my TV and computer. It had Romans 12:2 on it and the date the media fast was over.

Do whatever it takes. Stay strong. It is going to be tough. Help your buds in the group. You can do it. No doubt. Run at the challenge full-speed and feel the burn of taking control of your mind.

See you tomorrow.

['Cause what consumes your thoughts controls your life]
-- CREED, "WHAT IF"

Jumping out of a perfectly good airplane with an oversized bed sheet strapped to your back. It's called skydiving. I call it S.T.U.P.I.D. But hey, call me stupid, I had to try it.

A group of us went together. We climbed into the plane and cruised up to altitude. We each had an instructor strapped to us so we couldn't mess up too badly. The one thing the instructors repeated over and over was, "When we say jump...JUMP! Don't just half-way do it, but jump with all you got." See, here was the deal. The plane had a metal bar that went from the plane to the wing. You had to jump hard enough to get past the bar.

It was RJ's turn. He got up to the door and his instructor secured himself to RJ's back. Like they asked every jumper, the instructor shouted, "Are you in or out?" RJ shouted back, "I'm in!" 1, 2, 3, Jump! RJ hesitated. He didn't really jump. He just kind of let himself fall out of the plane. Remember the bar? RJ's foot hit the bar and spun them around. The instructor smacked against the doorway and sent them flipping towards the earth. The instructor recovered, gained control, and landed them safely.

The lead instructor turned around and looked at the rest of us waiting in the plane and shouted, "You're in or you're out! There is no middle ground!"

day 7

Get out your Bible, and check out Matthew 26:57-75.

THE WORD

Did you see it? Peter--did you see him? **He followed Jesus.**
But did you see it? He followed at a distance. This was the guy
who just a few ticks earlier was claiming, "I will die for you!" Now
he is close enough to see Jesus. But not close enough to touch Him.
Close enough to say, "I am in His sight," but not close
enough to say, "I am in His shadow." Oh yeah, Peter, that
sold-out believer who knew that Jesus was Savior, was not
committed enough to stand under pressure. Peter wasn't
in or out. **He was trying to live life in the middle.**

day·····7

LIFE LINK!

I know your works, that you are neither cold nor hot. I could wish you were cold or hot. So then, because you are lukewarm, and neither cold nor hot, I will spew you out of My mouth.

(Revelation 3:15-16)

You know the deal. Card. Write. Learn.

day 7

STEP OFF

Get in or get out.

Peter swallowed a jagged pill that day. He tasted the bitter lesson of Revelation 3:15-16. He learned that it is better to never follow Jesus than to follow Him and deny it. Peter wanted to commit, but not too much.

I know that it may seem like we're hounding this point. **But it is the issue of all issues when it comes to stepping off and living life over the edge.** This is the difference in going at it with full-on passion or just existing. You must be totally committed. Get in or get out.

34

day 7

What does it mean to really "get in"?
Two basic things.
Prayer. Bible study. Talking to God and reading His Word.

We'll get a close up look at those later. But for now, commit
to doing it. Right now, write a short prayer asking God to
help you commit to these two things. Tell the Father that you
want to jump. You want to get a total hook-up in knowing Him
more, and you are ready to STEP OFF.

lord, I pray you would help me to be
totally committed to you. Help me to learn
how to utilize Prayer & Bible study Properly

NO MEDIA?		PRAYER?
Yes		yes

Prayer

What is prayer?
Break it down in the simplest form.
Prayer is a conversation with God.

Why is praying so hard? Or why does it seem so weird? You can chat up your friends all day long. What's the deal with hablando (gringo, that means talking) with God?

What do you think?
Why do you feel it is so difficult to pray?

For me, it's because God doesn't have skin. I can't see Him with my eyes.
And I can't hear Him with my ears. It's hard for me to stay focused on talking with Him.

IS PRAYER IMPORTANT?

TEST:
When a war begins, what do our forces try to take out first?
a) the military leaders   b) communication methods   c) missiles, planes, artillery

ANSWER:
b) Communication.
   If they cannot communicate they
   are defeated.

SATAN KNOWS THIS. AND THE #1 THING THAT HE WANTS TO DO IS TO KEEP YOU FROM COMMUNICATING WITH THE FATHER.

day 08

What are some ways that you think Satan keeps you from praying?

The biggies for me are getting too busy and sleeping too late.

What about you?

✱ How do you pray? How do you focus on talking to a Father that you cannot see?

There are lots of "methods" people use. None of them are magic or make you super holy. They are just ways to help stay focused.

Some people use the word ACTS. The letters stand for words that give direction for praying:

  A--ADORATION
  C--CONFESSION
  T--THANKSGIVING
  S--SUPPLICATION

I use one that my youth minister taught me. PART. I added an "S" to make it PARTS.

  P--Praise
  A--Admit
  R--Request
  T--Thanks
  S--Shut Up

day 08

P-- Praise is all about God. Showing Him the love and telling Him how wonderful, powerful, and loving He is. It is singing to Him, shouting, dancing, just givin' it up for God. Telling people what we like about them is a good way to start any conversation. If you get stuck, read some of the Psalms. They are all about praisin' God in good and bad times.

"Praise the Lord!
For it is good to sing praises to our God
For it is pleasant, and praise is beautiful."
(Psalm 147:1)

A -- Admit the sins you have committed. This is where you tell God where you have messed up. The way I start this is I read Psalm 139:23-24. It says, "Search me, O God, and know my heart; Try me and know my anxieties; And see if there is any wicked way in me, And lead me in the way everlasting." I ask God to show me the things that I need to confess. (I am good at hiding or ignoring my sins). Hey, you pray this and mean it, and He will show you things-- so be ready. Ask for forgiveness and let God clean up your sin.

"If we confess our sins, He is faithful and just to forgive us our sins and to cleanse us from all unrighteousness." (1 John 1:9)

R -- Request stuff. This is where you ask God for things. Ask Him about things you need, want, and desire. Pray for things and ask for things for others. Be bold. He is our loving Father. He's a giver. So whatever it is, ask.

"Yet, you do not have because you do not ask." (James 4:2b)

T -- Thanks. Tell God thanks. Thanks for the cool stuff He has done. Thanks for trees, family, a raise, whatever. This is the time to tell God thanks for doing so much for you that you sure don't deserve. Gratitude is a beautiful thing.

"Oh, give thanks to the Lord, for He is good!" (Psalm 136:1)

day 08

S -- Shut Up! This is where you shut up and listen. Most people don't hear anything from God because they never stop talking. This is what really makes praying a conversation and not just a monologue to God.

"Be still, and know that I am God."
(Psalm 46:10a)

So that's the format I use. It helps me stay focused.

Let's unwrap a couple of other issues about prayer. First, get a prayer journal. Yeah this will help with the focus, but also it will record what you and your Father talk about. The way I do my journal is I break it up into five sections. One for each: Praise, Admit, Request, Thanks, and Shut Up. As I pray, I open up to the section and put the words down on paper.

I have friends who put everything on the same page and they use a different page every day. Hey, do whatever works for you. Mix it up. Don't just get into doing the same thing over and over. Snooze-fest! Make it fun. Try new things.

P Praise. Listen to praise music. Sing to the Father. Read Psalms or try to write your own. I write down what I know God is--powerful, loving, my Father, my strength when I am scared.

A Admit. I read Psalm 139:23-24. Write down the sins, the stuff you did that are not Christ-like. Then look at those things and think about how you got into the situations that allowed you to sin. Ask your Abba, your Dad, to forgive you.

R Request. Ask! Ask for big things, little things, everything. Write down what you ask and the date. Keep praying for those things until you get an answer. The reason to write it down is to know when it's answered. This way you remember to look for an answer. Then when you get the answer, write it down next to the request and the date it happened.

day 08

Important: Many people say, "God didn't answer my prayer," when what they mean is God didn't give them what they wanted. God can either say "yes," "no," or "wait." If He says "No", people get upset because God didn't answer their prayer. Yes He did. He said NO!

T Thanks. If something cool is happening, write it down and say thanks. Say thanks for simple things, your parents, your car. Walk around sometimes and look at nature. Throughout the day, look for things to say thanks about. My most-used prayer with God is "That was so cool, thanks."

S Shut Up. This is the hardest part but the most important. Sit with your pen and paper, turn the music off, and try to clear your mind of distractions. Ask the Holy Spirit to bring things to mind. Write down what comes. Read over your requests. Ask God what He thinks about each one. Read Scripture and write what pops in your mind. The more you do this, and the more you are quiet and listen, the more you will hear. God is talking. You will become more confident that what you are hearing is God. You'll be able to know what is Him and what is not.

This isn't some magical formula that gets you what you want. This is just how I do it. You don't have to do it like this. Find out what works for you. Know that any praying will be clumsy at first. Satan hopes you will get bummed and quit.

STEP OFF

Pray. Everyday. Commit to spend some time with God in a conversation. (That means He gets to talk too.) Don't let Satan break the communication. Get charged. Pray and STEP OFF.

REWIND:

THE TOUGHEST TIME WILL BE THE FIRST SEVEN DAYS. HANG IN THERE. IT WILL GET EASIER. --MEDIA FAST

day 9

BIBLE STUDY

What's that all about? Anything with the word **study** in it sounds boring to me.

I think the reason it's called Bible Study is because no one knows what else to call it. The Bible is not something to be studied the way you study your boring Biology textbook. **It is something to be explored.** It's interactive and responsive. It's more like you are surfin' the Bible rather than studying it. Hey, that's it. Bible Surfing. That's what we will call it. It is no longer Bible Study; it is now Bible Surfing.

Bible Surfing.
The Bible is an adventure. In it you will find sex, violence, hate, greed, love, power, forgiveness, compassion, winning the game against all odds, fighting 'til you can't fight any more, even saving a little boy from a government death warrant. It's all there.

In the middle of all these stories is a common theme, "Become Christ-like." The more you study--uh, I mean Surf--the more you surf the pages of the Bible, the more you understand about God.

41

THE WORD

Read Hebrews 5:11-6:3.

Get out the Word and read it.

This pretty much lays it out. When you are a new believer you need milk--and you need someone else to feed you. Hebrews said that when you first begin surfin' the Bible, it is OK to count on church pastors and Bible teachers to show you what's in there. But notice that it is also quick to say that you need to learn to feed yourself. You need to get into the Word on your own and stop being a baby.

So how do you do that? How do you start Bible Surfing on your own? People do it many different ways. I'll throw a few at you, and you find what works for you.

No matter how you surf, always start in prayer asking God to show you His truth in His Word.

TOPIC HOPPING

Think about a topic you are interested in: **Love. Friends. Sex. Forgiveness. Hope.** Whatever you want to know more about. Pick a topic. Then find as many verses talking about that topic as you can. Look in the concordance. (It should be in the back of your Bible, or go to the bookstore and grab an *Extreme A-Z: Find it in the Bible*.) There are also lots of sites on the Internet that will give you verses about topics. Ask your group leader to help you find a book that has topics connected with verses. Look up all the verses. Read what the Word says and write down what you get out of the verses. See how you can apply it to your life.

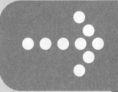

BOOK REVIEW

Pick a book in the Bible you want to surf through. Start at the beginning of the book. Find out who wrote it. Why did he write it? Where was he? (Some books were written from jail!) Start reading through the book asking questions about what's going on. If something catches your eye, look at it closer and find some other Scripture that tags that same issue. Read the whole book as a...well, as a book. Don't try to take one little piece and figure out what it means. Read it all so you can understand what is really going on.

PEOPLE WATCHING

Heard any interesting stories of people in the Bible? Look 'em up. Get to know them. How about David? He was a murderer, sexed up another dude's wife, got her pregnant, and was a poster boy for lying, yet God called David a man after His own heart. Why? How 'bout a trash-talking donkey? It's in there. Look up their stories. Learn from the lives of Bible people.

HEAD GAMES

Hey, this is important--memorize Scripture! When you see a verse that just rocks your world write it on a card. Get it in your head. This will help you in your real life. God uses those verses that you learn. He will bring them to the front of your brain when you need them. Don't ask me how it happens. It's a God thing, and He is in control of your circumstances and your thoughts. That is what the LIFE LINK! is all about. Getting the Word connected to your life.

DON'T GET IN A RUT. MIX IT UP TO KEEP IT FRESH.

Whichever way you are surfing through the Bible, constantly ask yourself questions:

Who? What? When? Where? Why? How?

Ask those about the author. Ask about what's going on. We miss a lot of what is going on in the story because we just read the words. Use your imagination. Try to see everything that is going on. Put yourself in the scene. If you were there, what would you be doing? How would you be acting?

Read the Bible from different perspectives.

Like the parable of the lost son who comes back home, read
it as if you were the son leaving. Try to see what he was
feeling and thinking. Then read it from the dad's point of
view. Then read it as the son who stayed behind. Feel the
way he felt. Then maybe read it from the view of the servants who worked for the father. There are so many view-
points in every story. See them all.

MAKE IT FUN. SURF THE BIBLE. RIDE THE
ADVENTURE. KNOW MORE ABOUT WHO GOD IS AND
WHO HE WANTS YOU TO BE.

Start now. Every day do some kind of Bible Surfing. It may be a little
weird at first. But, like the Word says, it is like learning to feed yourself.
You've seen a baby when he is just learning to use a spoon. Not the most
graceful thing. But he'll get better and so will you.

Write down a short prayer about Bible Surfing. Ask God to help you do
it, show you cool stuff and make it fun.
Start surfin' the adventure and STEP OFF.

_Lord I pray you would, help
me to search your word & learn
from it. Help me to see your
truth in it._

	NO MEDIA?		PRAYER?		BIBLE SURF?
	yes		_yes_		_yes_

day ¹⁰

High school football. Nothing like it. The smell of October in the air. The lights, the sounds, the frenzy. Oh, don't get me wrong. I never stepped foot on the field during a game. I may be stupid, but I'm not crazy. I am built like a popsicle stick with legs. Zero f-ball skills. But man could I talk. So I spent my Friday nights up in the press box. (We called it the bird's nest.) I would give fans the lowdown from up high.

My first game in the bird's nest I was chatting along, the door flew open, and there stood the coach. Wait, the coach? Wasn't he supposed to be on the field? I felt like I was on a crashing airplane and the pilot decided to step out for a moment. I shouted, "Coach, what are you doing here!?" He stared out onto the field and mumbled, "I needed a fresh perspective." I looked down at the sidelines and sure enough, chaos. Players and coaches running around. Band playing. Parents shouting. Cheerleaders cheering. Chaos. He needed to step out of the situation, get away from everything, come to the bird's nest, and get a fresh perspective.

THE WORD

Take a time out, and look up **Luke 5:12-15.** **Read it.**

Did you see the Friday night frenzy? Jesus was on the playing field. There were parents shouting for Jesus to touch their kids. There were cheerleaders cheering Him on. The assistant coaches (disciples) were running around giving orders. It was chaos. Jesus was right in the middle of it all. So what did he do? He took off to the "bird's nest." He needed a fresh perspective, so He got away from it all.

It was just Him and God.

Have you ever called time-out on your life to get a new perspective? Have you ever taken a 1/2 day and stepped away from it all? I don't mean get away to the mall or with your buds to the beach. **I mean just you and God?**

IF YOU HAVE   When was it? _____

Where'd you go? _____

What did you get out of it? _____

_____

_____

LIFE LINK!

Now in the morning, having risen a long while before daylight, He went out and departed to a solitary place; and there He prayed.
(Mark 1:35)

Write it down. Memorize it. Visualize it. See Jesus getting up in the morning, quietly sneaking out to pray.

STEP OFF

1/2 Day Getaway.

A good friend told me, **"Dude, if you're too busy to pray and spend time with God, you're just too busy."** He taught me to get away and spend time with just me and my Father.

Spend a 1/2 day away from everything with just you and God. Get alone, sing praise songs, pray, read the Word, talk with God, shut-up and listen to God. Write down the thoughts that come to your mind. Ask about things that are happening in your life. Tell Him what you think. Just be with your Dad.

Use what we talked about earlier: prayer and Bible Surfing.

This is going to take some planning. It isn't easy to get away by yourself for that long. But plan the time. It could be Saturday morning. Friday night. You pick the time. Look at you calendar now. Plan your time with God. What day are you going to do it? Where are you going to be? What are you taking with you? What time are you going to start and stop?

1/2 DAY CHECKLIST THIS WILL TOTALLY HELP YOU FOCUS ON THE FATHER.
Bible
Paper
Praise Music
Journal
Pen
Something to snack on—so you don't get hungry and distracted

What do you think will happen when you get away? What will be the biggest issues you have about actually doing it?

You are going be wow-ed by what will happen when you get a new perspective. This isn't going to be a one-time thing. Do it once a month. Set aside the time in advance. Plan next month's date now! That way when someone asks you to do something next Saturday morning, you can say, "Oh, I can't. I am hanging out with a friend of mine." **Make it happen.**

You have two days to figure out when, where, what, and all that stuff. Two days, so get planning. When you get with your group tell them about your plans. Ask them about theirs. (Don't make the 1/2 day a group thing though. It's a you and God thing.)

PLAN IT. DO IT. GET A NEW PERSPECTIVE. YOU WILL BE AMAZED. SO STEP OFF.

Rewind
How's your lifestyle? Are you still putting new life in a new lifestyle?
--Day 3

NO MEDIA?		PRAYER?		BIBLE SURF?
yes		yes		yes

DAY 11

You're cruisin' with your buds. You are looking at the directions and turn on what you think is the right street, only to realize that you are big-time lost. You look around the neighborhood, and there's graffiti splashed across every wall and sign. Windows are broken out of buildings, and there's trash in the streets. Homeless people are standing around a fire lit in a vacant lot. You are in the ghetto.

You keep watching. Everyone seems to look alike. They talk alike. They are staring at you, too, because they know that you don't belong there.

It's a city within a city. Stores, restaurants, houses, everything is there. No reason to ever leave the ghetto. They have their own ways, their own problems, their own rules. It is both security and a prison.

THE WORD

Don't miss what is happening. Christians have created their own ghetto. Think about that. Look at the story again and really think about it. A Christian Ghetto (C.G.). What would it look like? If there were actually a place, a Christian Ghetto, what would it look like? What would be the symbols, language? How would you know you were in the C.G.? What would the buildings, the people, and the streets look like?

We as Christians have created our own ghetto. We have our own Christian schools, Christian newspapers, TV shows. We have our own language, look, our own way of doing things. We don't even need to leave our Christian community. We have everything we need. We have separated ourselves from the world so that we don't have to venture out. We are safe in our ghetto. When strangers come around, we stare at them because we know they don't belong.

Check out the Word. Look up Matthew 9:9-13.

These religious people were flippin' out all over Jesus because he went out of the C.G. and was hangin' with people from another 'hood. The Word is so straight on. We are supposed to step out of our own little world and reach out to those around us.

LIFE LINK!

Go therefore and make disciples of all the nations, baptizing them in the name of the Father and of the Son and of the Holy Spirit.
(Matthew 28:19)

STEP OFF

Get out of the C.G.

Mix it up. We say we are going to change the world. How?
We go to Christian schools, Christian concerts, have Christian
friends. It's all "Christian." How are we going to change the
world, if we don't even know there's a real world?

So what now? Some questions.

What is the last thing you did that put yourself in contact with non-Christians. I
don't mean like you went to the mall shopping and there were probably some
there. But where you really got to trade vibes--connect.

Theatre

When was the last real conversation you had with someone who was not a
Christian? Ordering a value meal doesn't count. I mean, when did you last get
past the superficial Hollywood acting job everyone fronts and really get deep?

Saturday (1-18-03)

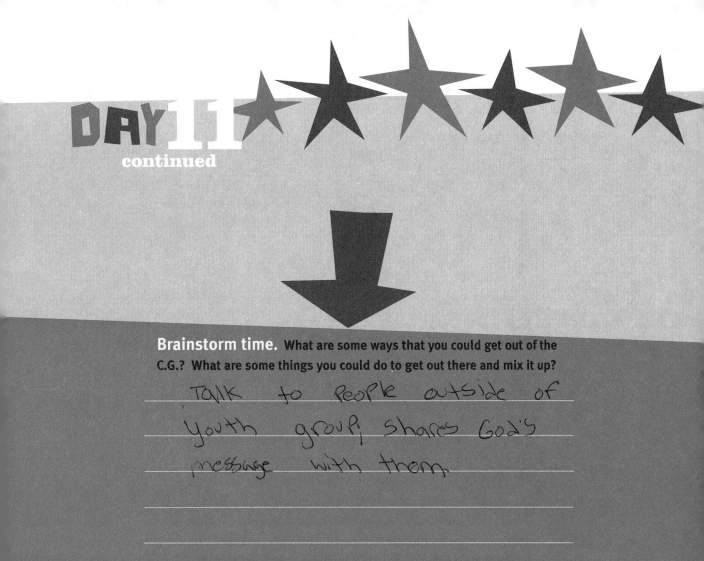

Brainstorm time. What are some ways that you could get out of the C.G.? What are some things you could do to get out there and mix it up?

Talk to people outside of youth group; shares God's message with them.

What's our deal? Are we supposed to witness to the saved or the lost? Don't be so Christian that you forget about the world! Take Christ to them--STEP OFF.

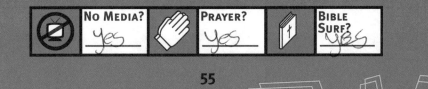

NO MEDIA?		PRAYER?		BIBLE SURF?
yes		yes		yes

day12

I was speaking at a large high school in Texas. After the assemblies I went outside to just chill and chat. I saw this guy that I just had to talk to. He said his name was Eddie.

Eddie was wacked. He had on shorts that came down below his knees with red and blue striped socks that were pulled up over his knees. He was wearing a sweatshirt turned inside out with a stick figure spray painted on it. His hair was long and shaggy and stuck out from a knitted hat that hung down to his waist. I looked Eddie over and asked, "Why do you dress like this?" Eddie smiled and said, "Uh, dude, I just want to be different." I looked over Eddie's shoulder, and there were eight guys standing there that looked just like him. I said, "How are you different? Those guys look just like you."

THE WORD

You become who you hang out with most.

Jesus spent his days with the "sinners." He reached out to them. The druggies, the whores, the drunks, the thieves, the bar hoppers, the lonely, the helpless--He wanted to touch all of them. He hung out in their neighborhoods and went to where they were.

But Jesus spent most of his time with twelve guys.
Out of those twelve, only 3 were in his inner circle. **Read Luke 9:28-36.**

Did you catch it? God was about to show the world who Jesus really was. Jesus knew what was about to happen, and He took his best buds with Him. Peter, James, and John.

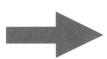

These guys were His closest friends. Jesus was tight with these three guys, because He knew they were sold-out followers. No, they weren't perfect, but they believed Jesus and wanted others to know Him.

Did you connect the dots and see what is happening? Jesus' best friends were Christians. Yeah, He would hang out with non-Christians, but the guys closest to Him were believers.

LIFE LINK!

Do not be misled: "Bad company corrupts good character."
(I Corinthians 15:33, NIV)

Card it. Make it mental.

STEP OFF
FRIEND CHECK!

● ●

Who are your best friends?

Christians: Talor & Tyler

Who do you spend most of your time with? Share your secrets with?

My best friends (Taylor, Tyler)

Who knows you inside and out?

Taylor & Tyler

Are they Christians?

Yes

Are they sold-out, full-on followers of Christ?

Yes

See, all of the disciples were followers. But Jesus' best friends were not just followers, they were living in total abandonment, stepping off, and following Christ.

Ready for the hard stuff? Take a friend-ventory. If your closest friends are not believers, or they are believers but don't act like it, you need to rethink the relationship. Read the LIFE LINK! verse again. How do you think that relates to your friends?

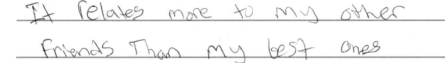

It relates more to my other friends Than my best ones

If your major pals are not Christians, they will bring you down. Hey the Word doesn't say, "Good company will change bad character." No, it's the total flip side. The Word is truth. It's real. Don't ignore it just because it's hard. **Check your friends.**

So what now? If you know that one of your deep friends is not following Christ with all they have, then you need to move them down on the friend food chain. That doesn't mean totally dis' them and bounce them from the ranks of bud. What it means is stop spending so much time with them. You can't open up your heart and ask for their honest advice, because what they say is not coming from God. Spend more time with solid believers. Get to know them in a deep core way so that you can help each other.

day 12

No, this isn't going against what we said yesterday.
Think about it. Connect the dots. Struggle with the idea.
Put them together and it makes sense.

Make sure you best buds are growing Christians so you can push each
other to be like Christ. Then, when you hang out with non-believers,
they can see Christ in you.

Make sense? **Prove it by doing it.**

	NO MEDIA?		PRAYER?		BIBLE SURF?		DAY GET AWAY?
	yes		*yes*		*yes*		*Not yes*

IF YOU CAN'T BEAT 'EM, JUST MESS WITH THEIR HEADS.

MINE! That's MINE! Some of the first words that kids learn. Everything...."Mine." People argue that when babies are born they are inno- cent and sweet. Whatever! Those people don't know the babies I know.

In kindergarten they teach you to share. It doesn't come naturally. It's all about Me. Mine. We are born selfish, and it gets worse from there.

Do something right now. Real quick, wherever you are, look around and see the things that are yours. If you are not in your room and can't get there to see your stuff, then visualize. Look at the stuff that is yours. Jot down a few of those things.

What do you own?

Guitar, Fan, Radio, TV, Bed

What are some things that are yours?

Same as above

THE WORD

Check out **Mathew 6:19-24.**

We try to get more and more stuff. The latest, the coolest, the best. First of all, it's not ours. Nothing in this world is really ours. We may have it with us at the moment, but the Word says that we are worried about collecting a bunch of junk. Second, it says that if we want to have a bunch of things, those things start to control us. We spend our time trying to get more, or we're worried that someone else will take what we have. We forget about God.

The Word tells us to store up things in heaven. How? The things we are doing here in Step Off are trying to teach us how to do that. We live the Word. All of it.

> ## ✱ LIFE LINK!
>
> And He said to them, "Take heed and beware of covetousness, for one's life does not consist in the abundance of the things he possesses."
> **(Luke 12:15)**

STEP OFF

What are some things that are really valuable to you? Not expensive, but the things you hate to even think about giving up. It could be a shirt, a stuffed animal, a football, a poster, whatever. Look around. Ask God to show you things that you have that you can't dream of losing.

Now, this may hurt: give it away! **That's right, give it away.** Whatever your thing was, find someone to give it to. (Don't go back and change your thing now. Don't be a pansy.) If it was a shirt, wrap it up, and give it away. If it was a childhood toy, same thing, find a kid to give it to. Ask your youth pastor or parents if you need help.

GIVE AWAY RULES

1 It has to be something that is YOURS. Don't give away a TV that belongs to your parents or a shirt that belongs to your sister.

2 Make sure that it is valuable to you! Not in $$$, but something you have a bond with. It can't be some blah thing that you think is just OK. It has to be something you really like.

3 Let it be a secret. Don't tell the person that it was you. Somehow, give 'em the gift and keep it on the down low.

Think about what is happening here. The real deal.

How do you feel about giving up something you really like?

I don't like the idea of it, its hard to see Something I like go.

What do you think about losing this thing?

I don't want to see it go

How do you think the person who ends up with your stuff will feel?

hopefully They will like it.

One more little sideline about the give-away. If possible, make it a top-secret mission. Don't let the person know where it came from or why they got it. Just do it. Don't tell a bunch of people, and if you give a shirt to someone that needs it in your school and they wear it, DO NOT tell your friends, "Hey look, he's wearing the shirt I gave him." Don't be a dork like that. Keep it a secret. Today isn't about the other person getting something.

It is about you letting go.

So let's break it down.

① Find something that is important to you.

② Search for someone or some organization to give it to.

③ Give it away.

It's that easy. And it's that hard! But hey, it's not yours anyway.
So give it up, and STEP OFF.

This bites. I am writing about giving away something that is really
meaningful. I looked up and there is Brown Bear. (That's his name,
don't laugh!) He's been my treasured bear since I was a boy. He has
been my friend, my compadre. We have solved many mysteries together
growing up. I looked up at him and heard the words, "He's gotta go."
Then my voice shouts in my head, "MINE!" It seems so stupid that I
have to give away my bear. But, God can use Brown Bear in another
kid's life to help him through tough times. He's a tough bear. He can
handle it. But can I? Good-bye Brown Bear.

WHATEVER YOU CAN'T GIVE UP CONTROLS YOU.

	NO MEDIA?		PRAYER?		BIBLE SURF?
	yes		*yes*		*yes*

day 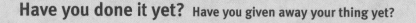 14

Have you done it yet? Have you given away your thing yet?

yes

Yes! That is excellent. God is so loving on you for having the guts to follow through, and I am stoked for you.

Hey, how'd it feel?

It felt very good

Who did you give it to?

A friend named Josh

How did it feel when you did it?

I was surprised How good it felt

What was the coolest thing about them NOT knowing where it came from?
The way you really felt, was it different from how you thought you would feel?

They don't have to feel embarrassed about it. I thought I would be sad, but I was actually excited

day • • • 14

No. You haven't given away your thing? Why not?

THERE ARE 3 MAIN ISSUES WHY YOU HAVEN'T DONE IT YET.

1) Selfishness

You may argue, "I'm not selfish. I just don't want to do it." That's called SELFISH. (Duh!) Selfishness will destroy you. If you cannot give away one thing to someone else, then how do you think you can follow Christ? He asked His disciples to drop everything. I'm asking you to let go of that death grip you have on just one thing.

2) Can't decide what

If you haven't figured out what to give, you're sticking to the wrong bubble gum. Move on! The what is not the important thing. The news flash is that you do it. If you are truly having a decision dilemma then hook up with your group leader, or parents, or somebody that will help you make the choice and move on.

67

day 14

3) Haven't found who

OK, I can dig it. It's only been a day. But don't let that excuse become
your cop out. Find someone to give to. If you are having trouble, then ask
your school counselor, ask your parents, friends, pastor. Look around the
neighborhood or your school. There are people around you every day that
could use and enjoy your gift.

> **WE HAVE TAKEN AWAY THE BIG 3 EXCUSES.
> ALL THAT'S LEFT IS TO LET GO AND MAKE IT HAPPEN.**

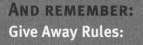

day· · · ·**14**

AND REMEMBER:
Give Away Rules:

- **It has to be something that is YOURS.** Don't give away a TV that belongs to your parents or a shirt that belongs to your sister.

- **Make sure that it is valuable to you!** Not in $$$, but something you have a bond with. It can't be some blah thing that you think is just OK. It has to be something you really like.

- **Let it be a secret.** Don't tell the person that it was you. Somehow, give 'em the gift and keep it on the down low.

As soon as you give away your thing, go back and answer the questions at the beginning.

day ·· 14

This isn't a one shot thing. Look around every once in a while. Find something you really like, and give it away. Hey, if you like it someone else will too. Loosen your grip on the things of this world, and you will be able to STEP OFF without hanging on.

REWIND
Pray for your buds.
Ask God to keep them tough in the media fast battle.

NO MEDIA? *yes*   PRAYER? *yes*   BIBLE SURF? *yes*   GIFT AWAY? *yes*

day 15

Who are these people?
I don't know

What are they doing?
Posing for a picture?

Where are they going?
To heaven hopefully

Where do they live?
On Earth, most likely

Are they friends?
hard to say, but probably

What are their families like?
Sad that they are related to them

Are they happy, sad, upset, worried?
Yes; each one has a different expression

What were they like when they were kids? (goodie-goodie, cool, shy, popular, geeky)
I going to have to go with geeky

day 15

Fill in the blanks. Don't just power past the story behind the picture. Look deep into the picture beyond what you see.

This may seem like a brain tease, but it is so much more than that. Click back to where we were talking about Bible Surfing. That is what today is about. Digging deeper, asking questions, and finding answers.

The Word paints a picture of what is going on, much like the one above. But if you don't ask questions to get behind the scenes, then you are missing out on the real story. Ask questions. Fill in the blanks and see how the Scripture comes to life.

READ ACTS 3:1-10.

Why did he sit in front of the gate that went to the church?

He was crippled & that is where he went to beg.

His friends brought him to the gate. Did they get a cut of the profits?

It doesn't say.

The beggar went there every day.
Do you think he got to know people by name?

Some, maybe, The ones that were compassionate enough to stop & talk

Peter said, "I don't have any money, but let me talk to you." Do you think the beggar heard that before?

Probably not, he most likely heard the money part, but not the talking part.

Do you think the beggar heard, "God bless you" from a lot of people who never gave him money?

Yes. People throw that around not realizing that God can Bless Them Through you.

This dude had never walked. What do you think it was like to walk for the first time as a grown man, not as a baby?

It said he leaped. I imagine God gave him the ability and strength at the same time

He had never seen the world above knee level. What do you think he could see now that he had never been able to see before?

He could look People in the as and talk to them as an eaual

The beggar was now walking. He ran, jumped, and praised God in the temple. What were the church regulars thinking when they saw the man?

They were in awe and wanted to know more.

What about those people who had made fun of the crippled man for years? The ones who laughed, played jokes on him, and just walked on by pretending the beggar didn't even exist. What was their reaction when the beggar looked them eye to eye in the church?

They Probably felt ashamed

What do you think the guy did for a job? He couldn't beg anymore. What skills do you think he had after sitting by the gate every day?

he learned to talk to People and take rejection, He Probably went on Sharing God's word with others

What would you do first if you had sat in front of the church and begged your whole life and, blam, you're healed?

Praise God and Tell everyone in hearing distance of his Glory.

day 15

Answer the questions. Think of the details of the beggar's life. After you have filled in the Q's, read the story in Acts again. See how it starts to pop and come to life. This is what Bible Surfing is about--allowing the Scripture to jump off the page and become an interactive story.

Get ready for the ride of your life. You will see the Word begin to breathe, live, and change who you are. Get in. Ask questions. **STEP OFF.**

NO MEDIA?		PRAYER?		BIBLE SURF?
Yes		Yes		Yes

day16

Carli and I went out on an awesome date. Our fave restaurant is named The Vision. Most incredible food ever. It's that froufrou food that looks really cool on the plate and they give you lots of it. Totally cool band playing salsa music. The atmosphere was incredible. We had starved ourselves all day in anticipation of the evening. We looked at the menu, each selecting our favorite and agreeing to share. We talked and laughed as we waited for the food to come. When it came...Omigosh!!! It looked even better than we had imagined. The aroma was playing "ring around the rosie" with my nose. The waiter asked if we needed anything else. **How do you add to perfection? The perfect food. The perfect music. The perfect night. The perfect date. Carli and I sat and admired the food for a while. Then, we paid the bill and left.**

THE WORD

Great evening. Right? What's the problem? No, you didn't miss anything. Read it again. We left. What? You think we are freaks? Probably so. No one would go to their favorite restaurant, order their fave dish, and just look at it.

Well, God's Word agrees with you.

Check it out. **Song of Songs (or the Song of Solomon, same thing) 2:7 and 3:5 and 8:4. It's in the Old Testament.**

Read all three verses.

If you were gonna guess what that means, what would you say?
Scribe it.
C'mon. Take a guess.

Don't Tease

OK, I don't know about you, but I don't have a clue about the whole "gazelle" and "doe of the field" bit. But the second part is pretty clear. "Don't tease me!" Don't take me to my favorite restaurant, set food in front of me, and then not let me eat it.

Do you agree that this would be stupid?.

A simple YES or NO will work.

Don't get confused here. This has absolutely nothing to do with what you eat.

See, it is so easy to get hooked on your crush. You date. You get comfortable. You trust each other. He won't make a move. She won't cross any lines. So you put yourself in situations that you shouldn't be in. The two biggies are the couch and the bed. And the Number One road to messin' up is, "We are just going to lay here and take a nap together." This is almost always followed by those words of promise:
"We won't do anything."

Why would you do that? (hint: stupidity) You and your crush alone, laying on the couch or in your bed, is like Carli and I in the restaurant. You check out the menu. You have this great babe dish and you are telling yourself you can't have it. You lay down. You enjoy the sight, the smell, the touch. This is awakening sexual desires in you. Then you are supposed to get up and walk away. Whatever.

YOU ARE IN A LOSE-LOSE SITUATION.

1. Guys, if you make a move then you a are a lying pervert who can't be trusted.

2. Girls, if the guy doesn't make a move, "He doesn't think I am pretty."
Either way you end up in loserville.

LIFE LINK!

But among you there must not be even a hint of sexual immorality, or of any kind of impurity, or of greed, because these are improper for God's holy people.
(Ephesians 5:3, NIV)

Memorize this verse. Make it a part of you.

STEP OFF

Commit!!! Make a commitment to not let there be a hint of sexual immorality. A lot of people commit to not having sex. But very few step off the edge into living Ephesians 5:3 full on. When you see yourself heading to a danger zone where there could be a hint of sexual immorality, then change plans, move locations—do whatever it takes.

WHAT ARE SOME WAYS THAT THERE COULD BE A HINT OF SEXUAL IMMORALITY?

1. Going to a backroom alone with your crush at a party.

2. Watching a movie at his (or her) house 'til 3 A.M.

WHAT ARE SOME OTHER PLACES?

Your house

WHAT ARE SOME OTHER SITUATIONS?

School, movies, anywhere

WHAT ABOUT THE CLOTHES YOU WEAR?

Be careful

Look at the stuff you wrote. Now it is time to really commit. Yes, commit to saving sex until you are married. But even more important, commit to not putting yourself in situations where there can even be a hint of anything sexual going on.

WRITE DOWN WHAT YOU ARE COMMITTING TO. TELL GOD WHAT YOUR DEAL IS WITH HIM. READ THE LIFE LINK! VERSE.

Lord, I commit to not having any sexual immortality until I'm married.

Take your commitment seriously, and live it for real. Take control of your life and start living all of the Bible, not just the easy parts, and STEP OFF.

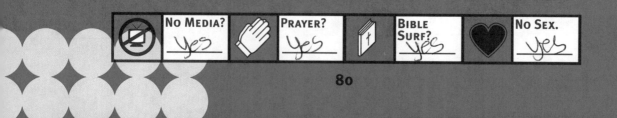

	NO MEDIA?		PRAYER?		BIBLE SURF?		NO SEX.
	Yes		_Yes_		_yes_		_yes_

Dr. Joy Browne. Ever heard of her? You have probably heard her on the radio. She has one of those radio talk shows where people call in and get advice. She wrote a book called "Dating for Dummies." In it she talks about something that blew me away. She wrote, I used to do a program in San Francisco, where people could vote on various questions--yes or no, pro or con. One day, I asked, "If you knew then what you know now, would you have waited longer to have sex?"

Fully 93 percent of both men and women resoundingly responded yes, they would wait....

A sobering thought, yes.

day ¹⁷
{continued}

LIFE LINK!

But among you there must not be even a hint of sexual immorality, or of any kind of impurity, or of greed, because these are improper for God's holy people.
(Ephesians 5:3, NIV)

STEP OFF

Remember the symbol stuff we talked about earlier? Why are symbols so cool for us to use? Do they make us do anything? Then what do they do?

Today I want us to make a symbol about what we talked about yesterday. This commitment about not even being around a hint of sexual impurity is so very important. So, today is a symbol day. Get a symbol of your commitment. Whatever works for you. Something you can see that will be a good brain-jogger.

For me, I use the ring with the cross on it.
Remember, I am the junk jewelry king. I bought my girlfriend
and myself the same ring. We went to dinner and had a cool
evening. Then we sat and talked about sex and what a hint of
sexual impurity looked like. (You've gotta talk about it before
the mood hits, because after that it's too late.) I gave her a
ring and put on my ring. We read the LIFE LINK! verse. And we
prayed to our Father. We made the deal with Him, and we wore
the symbol to remind us of our commitment.

Guess what? It worked! If I let my hands do some exploring, the ring
was there. It always made me think about the commitment. **Were there
times I wanted to take it off and forget the deal?** Oh Yeah! But I
couldn't without breaking my Promise (and the mood).

IMPORTANT MESSAGE FROM OUR SPONSORS:

Notice, I made a commitment to God, not to my gf. Why do you think that is important to remember?

God is our father and he wants us to be commited to him. Plus relationships don't always last

Oh, take a guess. Write something down. Anything. You can guess, "I don't know," or "Worms taste like chicken." Anything. Write it down.

Thanks. And yes, the reason it was so important that my deal was with God was **because me and my crush are no longer "us."** We broke up a while ago. If my commitment was to her, then breaking up would be a deal breaker and everything would be off. But my commitment was with God, and He isn't a deal breaker. So I still have the ring. And it still reminds me of Ephesians 5:3 every morning when I put it on.

GET WITH YOUR GROUP AND COMPARE **NOTES.**

Brainstorm on as many situations and places that could be danger zones.

Commit. Make it real. Live the extreme Word of God, and STEP OFF.

	NO MEDIA?		PRAYER?			BIBLE SURF?		NO SEX.
	yes		yes			yes		yes

DAY 18

The most honorable man I have ever seen was in San Miguel de Allende, Mexico. I was sitting in an outdoor restaurant overlooking a garden in the center of town. In the corner there were four people sitting at a table with another table right next to them where their kids had been eating. The kids had already finished and were out playing in the garden.

A little five-year-old boy walked up to the table where the children had been sitting. He could see a whole piece of pizza the children had left. (I recognized the boy. He was a little beggar boy that I had seen around town.) He asked the adults if he could have the pizza. They said yes, so he crawled up in the chair, took a napkin, and spread it out on the table. The boy took a big bite out of the pizza, then laid it on the napkin, and gently wrapped it around the slice. He moved the pizza to the edge of the table, got down out of the chair, reached up, and grabbed the pizza, and ran over behind a shop. (I could see behind the shop. He was taking the food to his mother and two sisters.) He came back and asked if he could have a bottle of Coke the kids had left. He did the same thing. He got in the chair, took a big drink, jumped down, and took it around to his family.

The boy made two more trips asking for food and taking it out to his fam. On the fifth mission he ran up to the table, but the adults were gone. He could see that there was more food left on the table that the kids had not touched. He looked around for the people hoping to see them. He took one last look at the food on the table, turned, and walked out without touching a thing.

I asked the waiter what the deal was, why didn't the boy take the food, especially since there was no one around? The waiter replied, "Sir, that boy is an honorable man. He is a beggar, he is not a thief."

THE WORD ●

Daniel 6:1-28. Read the whole story, it is way cool.

Isn't that incredible? The king made a law that said you pray to the king or die. What did Daniel do? He went up to his room to pray to God like he always did.

But wait. Did you catch verse 10? Daniel went upstairs to pray with the windows open. This is the character issue. Here is where the compromise tries to sneak in. See, Daniel could have gone inside and hid. He could have prayed where no one could see him. What's the big deal? He could still pray and no one would ever know. He could pray and not get in trouble.

The voice of compromise. Can't you hear it? Daniel could. In his head you know the thoughts were zinging around. Hey, it's only thirty days. I could just not pray to anyone. Just hold off and let the thirty days blow over and then kick up the praying again. I'm not going to pray to the king. So I just won't pray at all. It's thirty days. What's the big deal?"

The big deal was that it's a character issue. The little compromises that we think are "no big deal" are HUGE deals. They are telling us to compromise our character.

"Oh, it's OK to cheat on the test. I know the answers anyway. Besides, it's not like I killed anyone."

"I just wore the dress to the dance. I left the tags on it so I could take it back. No one will ever know."

"Yeah, I told my parents I was spending the night with my best gal pal so that I could stay out all night with my boyfriend. What's the big deal?"

IT'S A CHARACTER ISSUE! ●

LIFE LINK!

But the king spoke, saying to Daniel, "Your God, whom
you serve continually, He will deliver you."
(Daniel 6:16b)

WRITE IT ON A CARD. MEMORIZE IT.

STEP OFF
CHARACTER QUIZ (circle your answer)

1. You are hungry and have to help feed your family because they are starving. You:
   a. steal money or food.
   b. get on government programs that will get you money or food.
   c. get another job. Work more hours. Do whatever it takes to help your family.

2. You forgot about the big test that is going to count for half your grade. You:
   a. take the test and do the best you can.
   b. cheat off your classmate's paper.
   c. skip class and take the makeup, even though it will be harder and an
      automatic 25 points off.

3. You're at a party and your friends bring out the booze. You:
   a. call your parents to come pick you up.
   b. stay at the party but don't drink anything.
   c. tap the keg and drink 'til you puke.

4. Your bud lied to his parents and said he spent the night at your house then stayed out
   all night with his gf. His parents ask you about it. You:
   a. lie and cover for him.
   b. tell the truth.
   c. change the subject then tell him to come clean.

SCORING

1)	a. 1	b. 2	c. 3
2)	a. 3	b. 1	c. 2
3)	a. 3	b. 2	c. 1
4)	a. 1	b. 3	c. 2

CORE CHARACTER
(10-12 points)

Unquestionable character is your goal. You make decisions based on your convictions and what you know is right. Not what you feel. Your core is focused on being Christ-like, not on being liked by the world. Sometimes you get hurt or lose a friend because of your unbendable character, but hang in there. You are being shaped into the image of God. Don't get discouraged if you slip. You are not going to be perfect, but your commitment will make you, and those around you, stronger.

COMFORTABLE CHARACTER
(7-9 points)

You understand that character is important. You know how to make good choices. Some are based on your convictions; some are based on your emotions. You want to do what is right as long as it doesn't put you out too much. If there is too much of a commitment or a strain, then you would rather compromise your character than deal with the consequences. Build up your character one choice at a time. Your character will be stronger and so will your relationship with others and God.

CANCELLED CHARACTER
(4-6 points)

Sometimes it's easy to forget about our character. We are selfish people in a selfish world. We get caught up in winning and not in how we play the game. Character can be developed. You have to work at it. You have to be willing to get your feelings out of the way and make choices based on what is right, not what makes you feel good. Just like a cancelled check though, it will take some work to get out of the Cancelled Character hole. But you can do it. The payoff of solid character will be more than you dreamed.

These are character issues. Look at your LIFE LINK! verse again. It says, "He will deliver you." But you must realize that there are strings attached. God delivered Daniel because he did not compromise. He did not wuss out when things got hard. He stood tough and kept his character and won.

You make good choices. You really aren't a bad person, but you really haven't bought in to the truth that your character is important. You are willing to compromise on issues that make you uncomfortable.

What's your character? Are there places where you are compromising? You are not doing anything real bad, it's just something little: Lying. Cheating. Marijuana. It's not hurting anyone. What's the big deal?

Quit compromising! Stop saying, "What's the big deal?" Don't compromise your character even a little bit. Live with power, rage on, and STEP OFF.

GOD HAS NOT CALLED ME TO BE SUCCESSFUL. HE HAS CALLED ME TO BE FAITHFUL.
--MOTHER TERESA

REWIND

Have you gotten away with God yet? If so, how'd it go? What did you do? If not, quit slacking. Make it happen.

--Day 10

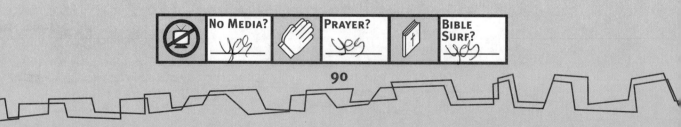

	NO MEDIA?		PRAYER?		BIBLE SURF?
🚫📺	yes	🤚	yes	✝	yes

day19

Most of us have never experienced real tragedy in our lives. Sure, we have bad things happen, but we have not had to go through what we would consider real tragedies.

What if you had to live through not one but two unthinkable tragedies? That is what happened to a man named W. Mitchell.

Mitchell was riding his motorcycle one minute, the next he was under a truck engulfed in flames. He had third degree burns over sixty-five percent of his body. Seriously disfigured, Mitchell fought back and succeeded. Four years later Mitchell was in a plane crash that left him paralyzed from the waist down.

Even after two major knock-out punches in life, W. Mitchell is one of the most positive people I have ever met. His attitude is incredible. Mitchell knows that your attitude is not how you feel. Your attitude is determined by your focus. In any situation you can focus on the good or the bad. If you want to change your attitude, you have to change your focus.

Mitchell says, "It's not what happens to you but what you do about it."

day19

THE WORD

Does this story sound remotely familiar? There was a guy in the Bible who seemed to be having a bad day, a bad week, a bad life. Take a look. Get out the Word and turn to Job 42:1-6.

Here's a rundown of what happened. Satan bet God that he could get Job to turn away from God. God said "Go for it! But you can't kill him."

Satan destroyed Job's children, servants, livestock, home, business, everything. Job stood strong. Then Satan tore down his body, and Job had sores all over his body. His wife told him to curse God and die. His friends accused him of making God mad.

Job held tight. He probably had some major Prozac days, but he never turned away from God. In Job 42:16, Job admitted to God that his focus was off. His attitude was bad because he was focusing on his bad situation and not on God.

Job was not happy about the pain and all the stuff that he went through. But Job changed his attitude. He had a good attitude because he changed his focus. He started looking for good in the middle of a bad deal. He found it, focused on it, and it changed his attitude. He changed his focus, and that changed his attitude.

LIFE LINK!

And we know that all things work together for good to those who love God, to those who are called according to His purpose.
(Romans 8:28)

92

day19

STEP OFF
Focus

It's not natural to find good in any situation. We were born with negativity radars. It takes practice to find the good. But once you get into the groove it will be automatic.

Time to STEP OFF and practice. Here is a story from Houston, Texas, reported by the Associated Press. Read it. Think about it. It is easy to see the bad. Keep looking and find the good. Write it down.

A 6-year-old girl was turning in papers at Youens Elementary School when she tripped and fell on her pencil. **The pencil went through her chest and pierced her heart.**

The pencil was not removed by teacher or firefighters. This girl was rushed to the hospital where the doctor said the pencil saved her life. If it had been removed the girl would have probably bled to death.

The girl is expected to be discharged from the hospital within two weeks.

FIND SOMETHING GOOD AND WRITE IT DOWN.

The pencil wasn't removed
from her heart and her
life was saved and she
will soon be discharged

> **SOME GOOD THINGS THAT I CAME UP WITH WERE:**
>
> --She's alive.
>
> --Everyone learned not to pull an object out of a person or he will bleed to death.
>
> --She has a wicked story to tell about her scare.
>
> --I didn't see it happen. (I would have passed out.)

Here's another one. It may take a little more to find something good. Again, this was taken from the AP.

A 57-year-old grandmother was sentenced to 25 years in prison for her role in beating, torturing, and killing a live-in friend she believed had molested an 8-year-old girl.

The man was found in front of the house he shared with the woman. He was in the middle of the street where he died from a severe beating during which he lost virtually all the blood in his body.

The prosecutor told the jury, "This (case) is about a guy who died because he was tortured to death, beaten to death, bled to death."

LOOK HARD. FIND SOMETHING GOOD AND WRITE IT DOWN.
YOU ARE ON YOUR OWN THIS TIME.

She wasn't sentenced to life; she has grandchildren.

Now it is time to take this attitude (focus) into your real life. The next time a teacher ticks you off, or a friend says something that scores high on the "mad-o-meter," or you hear about something bad happening, watch your attitude. Sure, your first reaction will probably be on the negative side, but remember attitude is your focus not your feeling. Look at the situation until you can find something good in it--no matter how big or small. Dig until you find something good to focus on.

CHANGE YOUR FOCUS. CHANGE YOUR ATTITUDE. STEP OFF.

IT'S ALL IN THE ATTITUDE.

REWIND
Have you given something away yet?
Did you go back and do Day 14? **Do it!**
--Day 13

	NO MEDIA?		PRAYER?		BIBLE SURF?
🚫	*yes*	🙏	*yes*	📖	*yes*

You did it! You made it through the Media Fast. See, it didn't kill you. You have just joined an elite club. Very few people in our nation are gutsy enough to try what you did, much less finish it.

We are so overloaded on media that we tend to forget about the real world. At the beginning of the Media Fast you answered some questions about the media and how you thought a fast would affect you. **Go back to those two original Media Fast days and check out the questions. Look at how you answered them. Let's go through some of them again and see how things changed.**

First: What was your LIFE LINK! verse?

Romans 12:2

When you were jonesing for that media fix, what did you do? How did you occupy your time?

Ate food, read, did Homework, Played guitar, worked out.

day 20

* You were asked what you thought would happen?
  Was that different than what really happened? How?

  I thought I would stop being so addicted, and it is true, I don't have a reall urge anymore

* Did you have a symbol? What was it?

  My Commitment Alter

* Did it help you? How?

  Yes, when I wanted to quit I would go look at it and remind myself

* What was your biggest urge to do?

  Watch the Superbowl

* What was the hardest thing to give up?

  Watching the Superbowl

* How did you fight the urge?

  I went to taylor's house and we hung out

★ What was the hardest part for you?

Not being able to plop down and watch T.V.

★ Were you more hooked on media than you thought? How so?

Yes. When I couldn't watch tv anymore, I realized how much I was hooked

★ What were you most hooked on? TV, movies?

TV & movies

★ Did it get easier as time went on?

Yes

★ Why was it so hard?

because everyone else in my family could watch tv.

★ Did your friends and family help you make it through? How so? What did they do?

Yes. They would help me stay focussed

What did you learn or experience through the Media Fast?

That I don't have to give in to an addiction and God will give you strength

Did the way you talked, what you thought about, or anything else seem to change about how you acted during the time?

Yes

What do you feel changed about you?

My whole attitude towards media and how addicting it can be

How do you feel about succeeding?

I feel awesome. God is great, he will always help us through.

You have just proved to your mind that you can do anything. You can control the urges in your head that shout to be heard. The voices that say you cannot exist without TV, movies, Internet. Anything else you are asked to do should be a breeze. Yeah, they may be hard, but you can do it. You just proved it.

Right now, do some PT (prayer time). Get with your Father and tell Him thanks for helping you get through the Media Fast. Talk to Him about all the things that He taught you through it. Write down some of the things that come to mind while talking with God.

Watch out. Now is a tricky time. Like when people go on a diet. They will starve for two weeks. They lose ten lbs. They are so happy. As soon as they get off their diet, they hit the restaurant and stuff their face like a sumo wrestler at an all-you-can-eat buffet. Then they are shocked that they gain twenty lbs. back. Duh.

Well be careful. Don't go on a media binge and soak up all the trash TV, music, and movies you can in 48 hrs. Chill. Take your time. See if you can use the past 21 days to help you cut back. Change your lifestyle. Change what you do. You will be amazed at what happens when you keep your mind in check.

 UNTIL NEXT TIME: CONTROL WHAT GOES IN YOUR HEAD AND
STEP OFF.

PRAYER? *yes*   BIBLE SURF? *yes*

day 21

Youth night at church. The teens actually got the chance to run the service. It was my job to deliver the message (ya know, like preach). Well, I got some of my friends together. We did a "what if" version of Moses and the burning bush. One dude was the bush, we had a guy doing the voice of God, Moses--we had it all. We asked a lot of "what if" questions. Like what if you were walking in the field by your house and there was a bush on fire. What would you do? (Yep, we squirted the bush with a fire extinguisher.) **It was a blast!**

After the service everyone was telling us how much they enjoyed the service. Everyone except the head deacon of the church. He walked up and just started flakin' out on us. "What do you think you were doing? How dare you do that in the House of God?" he shouted. We said, "Sir, we were telling the story and just having fun." Red-faced and bug-eyed the man yelled, "Boys, this is a church. **This is not a place to have fun!"**

THE WORD

Check it out. John 2:1-11. Read it, and picture the scene.

Where was Jesus? A wedding. Back in Bible days, a wedding was not just an hour-long ceremony with a quiet little reception. Oh no. It was a week-long event. Fiesta city! And Jesus got an invite. They wanted Jesus at the party. What does that mean? Let me ask you a question. Would you invite some boring, Bible-thumping geek to your party? Not me! Who wants a bunch of stiffs at a big bash?

Jesus was invited because He was liked. People liked having Him around. A lot of Christians forget (or just ignore) that Jesus' first recorded miracle was done at a wedding party.

Can you see it? Jesus was laughing, dancing, telling jokes, and enjoying the party. Someone yells, "Hey Jesus, come here. I want you to meet a friend of mine." Jesus was at a party, and He was having a blast.

LIFE LINK! *

You are the salt of the earth; but if the salt loses its flavor, how shall it be seasoned? It is then good for nothing but to be thrown out and trampled under foot by men.
(Matthew 5:13)

That is your LIFE LINK! verse. Write it on the card and learn it. But don't stop there. Read verses 13-16.

You are the salt of the earth; but if the salt loses its flavor, how shall it be seasoned? It is then good for nothing but to be thrown out and trampled under foot by men. You are the light of the world. A city that is set on a hill cannot be hidden. Nor do they light a lamp and put it under a basket, but on a lampstand, and it gives light to all who are in the house. Let your light so shine before men, that they may see your good works and glorify your Father in heaven.
(Matthew 5:13-16)

day 21

STEP OFF

Have Fun!

Don't buy into the lie that, if you are a Christian, you have to be "straight laced" and boring. Look at the LIFE LINK. It says that we are supposed to be the "salt of the earth." That means we are supposed to make people thirsty to know Christ. They should look at us and want to be like us. They want what we have--Jesus. If you are a snoozer, you'll make people thirst to get away from you.

SO HAVE FUN.

What are some things that you do that are fun?

Theatre, Football, being weird

Who is someone that makes you laugh?

Taylor Bartlett

What is something that you remember doing that was crazy fun?

Play jokes on People at the "River"/mall

What is something that you would like to do that you think would be fun? Why don't you do it?

learn to tapdance. No tengo mucho dinero

day 21

Somewhere we have been made to believe that Christian = Geek. Don't get all righteous on me now and tell me, "Oh, I don't think that." You know it happens. If you see someone that is on the edge of fashion and the life of the party, then you don't think about them being a believer. No, to be a Christian you have to dress like a dork, listen to crappy music, have no sense of humor, and sit around reading the Bible saying, "Praise the Lord," all the time. GET OVER IT!

Have fun. Learn some jokes. Read the comics. Go play on the merry-go-round. Bungee jump. Whatever. Christians should be the edgiest and most fun people around.

When you get together with your group, throw out ideas of fun things that you can do. Think of things that you and the group could do that would be a rush.

BE SALTY. MAKE PEOPLE THIRSTY FOR THE LIFE YOU LIVE, AND STEP OFF.

day
21

SALTY SUGGESTIONS

1. Read the newspaper. People will want to chat with you if you have more to talk about than Brad Pitt's bod or Jessica Simpson's curves.

2. Make others feel special. Cards, phone calls, and e-mails are always big winners. Ask questions and listen to the answers. Open the door for everyone.

3. Be creative. Write poetry, paint, sing. Cover your notebook in leaves. Shop at the thrift store. Creative people are attractive people.

4. Laugh. Laugh at yourself. Find humor around you. Even if it's not there, make up a funny story in your head. Learn some jokes. Watch funny flicks.

People will want to hang with you and will beg you to know your secret. They'll want to know the Jesus you have. And that's what being salty is all about.

PRAYER? Yes BIBLE SURF? yes

day 22

Ever been totally busted on something without saying a word? It's written all over your face. The way you're acting. The way you look. You're busted. Like if you kiss your gal pal's boyfriend, or you wreck your dad's car. You don't have to say anything, but somehow they know just by looking at you. Hey, it doesn't have to be something uncool. It could be on the good. You win the big game. She said she'd catch a flick with you on Friday. You get a raise. You are stoked, and everyone knows it. Most of the time our words are just agreeing with what our body and actions are already saying.

day 22

THE WORD

We get so caught up in words that we sometimes miss the real story. Check out Romans 1:18-20.

If you were gonna guess what this means, what would you guess?

No EXCUSES? God is Powerful

Well, check this out and see if it makes more sense. Psalm 19:1-4.

Nature shouts it out. It can't hide it. God is real. We miss it because we don't listen to nature. We are lazy. We want words. Nature says more without a word than that yakkity girl who sits behind you in English.

Nature is blabbin'. We can see so many cool things about God if we just pull our head out and listen to nature.

day 22

LIFE LINK!

For since the creation of the world God's invisible qualities--
His eternal power and divine nature--have been clearly seen,
being understood from what has been made, so that men are
without excuse.
(Romans 1:20, NIV)

STEP OFF

Go Natural!

Nature is telling the story of God. I didn't say that.
God's Word said that.

Look at nature. Look close. Trees, birds, wind, dogs, stars, rain.
Look at it, and listen to it. You will see cool things about God.
Who He is and how He acts.

day 22

1. Pray that God will show you cool stuff through His nature.

2. Find one thing in nature and focus on it. Pray. Look at it. Smell it. Feel it. Listen and see what is being said about God.

3. Every day this week, all seven of them, find something different in nature. See what it is saying about God. It may be as simple as seeing a flower and seeing the beauty of the Father, or as complex as seeing an anthill and thinking about how we must help our friends and family.

EVERY DAY, FIND SOMETHING IN NATURE AND ANSWER THESE QUESTIONS.

What is it?

What did you think this part of nature is saying about God?

What could that have to do with your life?

Do this every day for the next seven days.

That means do it now. Find something in nature. **Right now.** No matter how big or small and answer the questions.

God is so cool. He is showing me things that are pushing me to STEP OFF.

day ● ○ 22 ○ ●

I was sitting in the parking lot of a grocery store. It was raining so hard that I could barely see out the window. But what I did see was incredible. There were two inches of water flowing over the entire parking lot and down into the sewer. The thing I noticed was that there was no trash in the parking lot. Nothing. No cups, no paper, no cans, nothing. Everything was floating away. The trash was being washed away.

I started thinking about that, and God showed me some incredible stuff. (It had to be God; I'm not that smart.) The rain was like God's forgiveness. When we ask our Father to forgive us, He does. His forgiveness flows over us and washes all of the trash out of our lives.

Wow! I was blown away. I sat in the car listening to the rain and thanked God for forgiving me and washing the trash out of my life.

	PRAYER?		BIBLE SURF?		NATURE?
	yes		yes		yes

day 23

KNOW YOUR FUTURE.

Know your soul.

Answers to questions you
didn't know to ask.

SCORPIO (October 23-November 21)
With your place on the zodiac you are unstoppable. The world is your playground.
The good winds of adventure blow your way. But beware of Pisces. Too much
interaction can alter your skyward course.

SAGITTARIUS (November 22-December 21)
Festivals of love will renew your spirit. If the future gets foggy and you can't see
clearly the intentions of your crush, look to the full moon for guidance.

CAPRICORN (December 22-January 19)
Lots of academic success awaits you thanks to Venus. Don't stress about last
minute efforts to gain a point or two. Your stars have you covered.

AQUARIUS (January 20-February 18)
You can count on the counsel of friends you would least expect to turn to. Do not
be surprised if they use more alternative means to finding the solutions.

PISCES (February 19-March 20)
Caution. The Neptune moon has you on its hit list. Failure in social settings is
imminent until the 15th, when an Aquarius will deliver you from your isolation.

ARIES (March 21-April 19)

Cosmic omens reveal your distraction when looking in the mirror. Utilize charismatic Jupiter to enhance qualities that already exist within your spirit. The 3rd will be most intense in your self-realization.

TAURUS (April 20-May 20)

Open your mind and explore the possibilities. Your tunnel vision has held you captive with chains of ambiguity. Break free. Aquarius will make a good ally for your journey.

GEMINI (May 21-June 21)

An ongoing family struggle threatens to interfere with inner harmony. Right the fight using the forces of Mercury, the planet of intelligence and communication.

CANCER (June 22-July 22)

The fitness enthusiasm of your inner self has you gym hopping from the 8th-14th. Use this energy to defend against looming laziness between the 15th-22nd.

LEO (July 23-August 22)

Forced to decide which road to travel in a tough situation. Leo must not be ruled by the Sun, instead use your natural decisiveness to pounce on opportunity.

VIRGO (August 23-September 22)

Gemini throws you a curve. Your usual disposition is becoming more sensitive. This will prove useful on the 18th. Take time to enjoy the friends you have.

LIBRA (September 23-October 22)

A voice from the past rekindles old memories. You are faced with a dilemma. Look to Venus, the planet of love and pleasure, to help you sort out emotional emergency from true love.

Before you plan your life around your horoscope, I have a confession. I made that stuff up. That's right! Just a bunch of yadda put down on paper.

Many people are into this whole psycho, uh...I mean psychic, thing. What's your birth year? What's your zodiac? Where's your brain!!? They think it's no biggie and it must not be too bad because it's in all the mags. Those same magazines tell you how to do your boyfriend but that doesn't mean it's OK!

With fortune-tellers and horoscopes, you have two choices:
1. These people are for real. They actually use spirits to see things. If that's true, in the Bible days, these people would have been killed. Leviticus pretty much lays it out. If you want to talk to the dead, we will make you dead.

2. These guys are full of crap. The sad thing is that people are so needy they will believe anything.

So, if you are one of those people who consults your horoscope to get the lowdown, either you are dabbling with demons or you're a sucker. Either way, you lose.

THE WORD

The Word is clear. Deuteronomy 18:9-13.
Read it.

Horoscopes, late night psychic hotlines, ouija boards, séances: these are not just games. They are serious issues. God demands that we stay away from that kind of stuff. These are all toying with demonic forces. Our Father, who knows everything about our future, is trying to protect us.

Pray that God will help you recognize things that are from the demonic side.

LIFE LINK!

For I know the thoughts that I think toward you, says the Lord, thoughts of peace and not of evil, to give you a future and a hope. (Jeremiah 29:11)

Write it. Learn it. Believe it.

STEP OFF

Read your Holyscope. (I know that is high on the cheese-factor, but work with me.)

Check out these words about your life and future and some just random things:

Don't look on wine when it is red, when it sparkles in the cup, when it swirls around smoothly, because in the end it bites like a serpent and stings like a viper. Your eyes will see strange things, and your mind will get twisted.

If you follow the emotions of your heart, you're a self-confident fool.
If you follow what you know is right you'll be a total success.

Don't be too cocky, it will destroy you. Try humility. It may mean you have to mix it up with a different crowd, but that's better then being popular and dead.

No I didn't make these up. And I didn't pull them off www.iamstupidforbelievingthis.com. No, actually all of these came from the Word. (They were taken from: Proverbs 23:31-34, Proverbs 28:26, Proverbs 16:18-19.) These were just random things that I flipped through and found.

If you really want to know what the future holds for you, then get off the horoscopes and get in the Word. Dig into the Scriptures. Start with Proverbs. Great wisdom. Keep searching. The answers are there.

I have a friend who says, "I need to go read my horoscope," and she picks up her Bible. God knows your future. He will let His Holy Spirit reveal the secrets to you when the time is right. Until then, stick to the Bible for your guidance and to consulting the One who put that love line on your hand--God. And STEP OFF.

	PRAYER?		BIBLE SURF?		NATURE?
	_____		_____		_____

IF YOU ARE GOING TO CALL IT LIKE YOU SEE IT, YOU HAVE TO SEE IT LIKE IT IS.

day²⁴

This homeless man walked into church one Sunday morning.
He looked a little nervous as he slowly walked down the aisle and found a
seat. He tried to smile and say hello to people, but everyone would look
away as soon as he made eye contact. He was wearing dirty pants, his
shoes had no shoe laces, his coat was ripped, his shirt stained, and he
smelled a little like raw fish.

> The man walked halfway down the center aisle and took his seat.
> Immediately, the well-dressed church members sitting next to him
> got their children and moved.

In the back, the ushers were having an emergency meeting to try to figure
out what to do. See, this wasn't just any Sunday. This was the Sunday a
new preacher that the church wanted to hire was coming to preach. The
church wanted to make a good impression and show the preacher that this
was the kind of church he wanted to lead. Now there was a homeless man
sitting right in the middle of the church messing things up.

The ushers decided something had to be done. The lead usher
walked up to the man. (The homeless man had now taken out an apple
and begun to eat it.) The usher asked in a soft yet stern voice, "Sir, may I
help you?" The homeless man smiled and simply said, "No thank you."
The usher quickly asked, "Wouldn't you be more comfortable in the
back?" "No, I'm OK here." Finally the usher said, "This is an important
day. I need you to please go sit in the back. We have found a good seat
for you back there."

The homeless man knew what the usher was saying. He gathered up his things and put them back in his bag. He got up and sadly walked to the back of the church.

The service began. A man stood up in a very nice suit and announced that the church had offered someone the Senior Pastor position, and he was there to speak in the morning service. He asked everyone to please welcome David Swinson.

The crowd began to applaud. The homeless man stood up and walked down the center aisle. The ushers didn't know what to do. The man walked straight up to the stage and took the microphone. He looked at the congregation and said, "My name is David Swinson. I came here this morning to accept the offer to be Senior Pastor. But after what I have experienced this morning, I have changed my mind."

Then David Swinson, the pastor, the rejected homeless man, walked out of the church.

THE WORD
Matthew 25:34-46.

Did you see it? Did you see the church members? Did you see the homeless guy? Did you see the guy in your homeroom class that no one talks to? Did you see the guy in the mall that sweeps up the trash? Did you see the people who stay the night at the Salvation Army? Did you see it? Did you see the ones Jesus called "the least of these"?

We lose sight of the real deal sometimes, and we think we can't see God. We feel like He is so far away from us. But He tells us right here in His Word that He is all around us, and if we give to others, we are giving to Him. If we are nice to others, we are nice to Him. We help others, and we are helping Him.

LIFE LINK!

I tell you the truth, whatever you did for one of the least of these brothers of mine, you did for me.
(Matthew 25:40, NIV)

Write it. Get it in your head.

STEP OFF

You can tell a lot about a person by watching the way he treats people who can do nothing for him. Yeah, it's easy to be nice to people who can help us. Someone who can get us in the club, give us the hook-up on the popular scene, has money and a car to cruise in. But if you really want to know about a person, watch how he treats the waiter at the restaurant. Listen to what he says when a homeless person asks for money. See how he acts when an uncool dude with no friends wants to sit with him at lunch.

It's easy to be nice to the uppity, but what really counts is how you treat people who have been beaten down by life and seem hopeless. See, Jesus didn't say "if you did it to the highest and most popular"; He said, "the least of these."

day²⁴
{continued}

What are some things that you can think of to do for "the least of these"?

-- WORK AT THE SOUP KITCHEN.

-- GO HANG OUT AT A NURSING HOME OR A CHILDREN'S HOSPITAL.

-- SLIP MONEY INTO THE LOCKER OF A POOR KID AT SCHOOL.

-- PAY FOR SOMEONE'S LUNCH WITHOUT THEM KNOWING.

> There are so many things that can be done. What are some things you can think of?

Talk to kids who don't have anyone to talk to at lunch

help out at church (cleaning)

1. Get a card. Think of a teacher who you don't like. Write something nice and positive on the card. Something like, "Mrs. Jones, thanks for your encouragement. You have impacted my life. Thanks!" Don't sign your name. Then sneak it on the teacher's desk without telling anyone.

2. Learn the janitor's name at school. Every morning when you see him, greet him by using his name. "Hey, Mr. Simms." It's that easy.

> These are two simple things that will make a huge difference in others. **Do it! Do it unto the least of these, and do it to Jesus.**
>
> Start looking for ways to help others. It doesn't matter how big or small it is. It just matters that you reach out and STEP OFF.

PRAYER? _yes_   BIBLE SURF? _yes_   NATURE? _yes_

DAY 25

FULL-ON ACTION DAY. TODAY IS ALL ABOUT GETTING
OFF THAT BOO-TAY AND DOING SOMETHING.

THREE THREES

3 messages

3 compliments

3 dollars

3 **Messages--**Sometime today send three different people a message. Use whatever you want. Shoot 'em an e-mail. Call them on the phone. Snail mail a card to them. Drop a note in their locker. Whatever. Just take the time to send them some good words.

MAKE IT SOMETHING SHORT AND SWEET.

"Hey, just thinking about you. You are a great friend. I am a better person because of knowing you."

Easy. No big deal to do.

You know how it feels when you get a groovy card in the mail. There is still something about having an envelope to tear open and a card inside. (That is my personal fave.) You know how cool it is to get a note from someone for no reason? Those are the best. So do that for someone else.

Check out my short example again. Notice, I didn't say, "call me back," "write back soon," or anything else that demanded a response. Those are strings attached. Don't ask for anything. Just give them some encouraging words and let it go.

3 Compliments--Give some ups to the people around you. Compliment them. Lift 'em up with your words. It's great to hear people tell you how good you are. Do it for others. Look around. You are going to bounce into a lot of opportunities to dish out the goods. And hey, teachers and parents are not off limits. Imagine what kind of brownie points you'll score by ravin' about Mrs. Johnson's new hairdo.

Pay attention to what you say. Compliment the person, not just a thing. Yeah, compliment someone's shirt, but say something like, "Hey, I like that shirt, it looks great on you." That way you hit the thing (shirt), but you tag him with a feel-good too.
(Caution: Don't be a fake. Everyone knows when you are not sincere.)

3 **Dollars--**Give it away. We can get give-happy with e-mails and compliments, you even gave away something that was precious to you, but it's time to hit where you live. **Money.**

Give away three dollars today. C'mon, it's only three bucks. (It has to be your money. Don't beg money from the parents to give. It has to be yours.) Give it to someone you think might need it. Don't just walk up to someone and hand him or her the coin and say, "Here, I think you need this." Have some tact. Give it on the sly. Stick it in a shoe during gym. Sneak it into an English book while no one is looking. Slide it in a locker. Find a way to give away the cash. Can you buy food for one of the people you see holding cardboard signs beside the street? YES. Take your money and get it into the life of someone else. To you it's only $3. To them it may mean the world.

333. It's all about others. We, as sold-out believers, should make 333 a habit. Everyday we should give a little of ourselves to help someone else. It could be as little as telling a new kid "hello" or as big as helping build a house for someone. Make 333 a part of your life. Every week plan a day for 3 messages, 3 compliments, 3 dollars and STEP OFF.

	PRAYER?		BIBLE SURF?		WRITE A NOTE?		LEARN JANITOR'S NAME
	yes		yes		No		yes

I KNOW GOD WILL NOT GIVE ME ANYTHING I CAN'T HANDLE.
I JUST WISH THAT HE DID NOT TRUST ME SO MUCH.
--MOTHER TERESA

ATTITUDE CHECK

A 26-year-old woman traded her daughter for crack.

The woman told the court that she had taken her daughter to the crack house and left her for the drug dealer. She said she did not know what happened to her daughter that weekend except for what her daughter had told her. The daughter told her mother that she did "favors" for the man all weekend.

In exchange for her daughter, the woman received $15 worth of crack cocaine.
The woman is now waiting to be sentenced in a child abuse and neglect case. The girl has been placed in foster care.

Remember the LIFE LINK! verse from a few days ago?

And we know that all things work together for good to those who love God, to those who are called according to His purpose.
(Romans 8:28)

Check your attitude. Remember, attitude is about focus not feelings. Yeah, we should feel bad about things like what happened to the little girl. If you don't, there may be something wrong. It's a horrible thing. But focus and find something good in this bad situation.

Write it down. Whatever you can find that is good, write it down.

> The girl might end up in a way better enviroment than with her mother

Now, look at your life. Here's an easy assignment. Think of three bad things that have happened to you or your family. Write them down. Take your time. Filter through the events of your life, find three downers, and write them.

1. Dad lost his Job
2. Mom had to go back 2 work
3. Liza needs braces, but we haven't been able to get them.

It gets a little more difficult. For each of the things that you wrote down, write down one thing good. Think about the whole picture of what happened. What do you think God could be showing you? How do you feel each bad event could help you become more Christ-like?

1. Dad might get a better Job

2. Mom might appreciate staying at home More

3. Some of Liza's teeth might straighten out themselves. (cheaper Dental Work)

Take this with you in the real world. **When something bad is going on, remember your attitude is determined by your focus. If someone hurts your feelings, you have a bad day, or a house burns down, then your reaction will probably be negative. Change your focus and change your attitude.**

Also remember, other people have bad days too. You don't have an "all-rights-reserved" on bad days. Things happen to other people. Their attitude could go straight down the toilet. What can you do? If someone else has a bummer of a time, what could you do to help them focus and change their attitude?

Help them see the good.

make them smile/laugh

listen & be compassionate

Here's a little "What If" to make it easier. What if a student in your biology class was upset because her sister was in a car wreck and is in the hospital paralyzed.

What can you do to help?

What can you do or say to help with the focus?

Write some things down. **Think about it.** Notes, words, whatever. Write down three things that you could do to could help.

You could tell the girl that you'n be Praying for her sister.
Tell her to be thankful her Sister is alive.
listen & Just be a shoulder to cry on, cheer her up

 We've looked at a lot of attitudes today. The story of the little girl. You looked at your life, thought of bad stuff and then found good.

You looked at someone else's bad day and thought about how to help her. It's time to take this where you live every day. You determine what you focus on, therefore you choose your attitude. Don't let your emotions control you; you control your emotions, and STEP OFF.

PRAYER?		BIBLE SURF?		NATURE?
yes		yes		yes

THE GREATEST DISCOVERY OF MY GENERATION IS THAT HUMAN BEINGS CAN ALTER THEIR LIFE BY ALTERING THEIR ATTITUDE OF MIND.
--WILLIAM JAMES

day 27

Tomorrow you die!

I know. You're too young. You haven't even really started living, but that's it. Your life is over.

The funeral: think about it. Your parents are there. Your family. Your friends and teachers. They are all standing there. All the people that have ever made a difference in your life are looking at your body thinking, "What if..."

Regrets? Have any?

Never made a difference, never led anyone to Christ, didn't live my life very long. Didn't tell a lot of people about Christ

What are you sad about?

Sad I won't see my family anymore.

You are hovering over your casket watching the scene.

What do you want to say?

I'm sorry for not always being Christ like.

What do you wish you could do?

Go back in time and change it

Let's watch everyone as they walk by and look at you. Let me dig in your business a little. Your mom and dad. What would you want them to know?

I'm sorry for not being the son I should have been

What do you wish you could say to them?

How much I love them

Would it be how much you loved them?

yes

Would it be that you're sorry for hurting them?

yes

What would you say to them or what would you do? Hug them? Spend time with them? What? Before you move on write it down.

I would hug them and Tell Them how Great they are

Your best friends. Write down their names.

Taylor, Tyler, Jacuves

Look at each name and think about them separately as they walk up and say good-bye. What do you wish you could tell them? (Remember: You're dead) What do you want them to know about how you felt about them?

I enjoyed being there friends

day
27

↙

What is something that you would have liked to have done with them that you never got to do? Write it.

Go Skydiving, Hang out more

Think about other people that have made a difference in your life. Who are some of those people? What would you like to tell them about what they meant to you?

My Grandpa; How much I love him.

What would you like to send to someone that you never sent? Card? Flowers?

Flowers

You're dead. You are looking down at your life. Answer this:

I regret not telling More People **that** Jesus loves Them .

I wish My Parents **would have known** How much I love Them .

I regret not doing More for christ; missionaries, work etc .

DON'T READ ANY FURTHER UNTIL YOU HAVE ANSWERED THESE QUESTIONS!!!

day 27

Read Matthew 8:18-22.

Did you connect the dots? Did you see what the Word said about the questions you were answering? Basically it said that dead means too late. If you are still alive, Game On! You still have a chance to impact lives.

Look at the stuff you wish you would have said or that you regret not doing. Think about what you missed and what they missed by not doing it.

Abracadabra and other goofy magic words! You're alive again. There you are reading this page. Hang with me. Go back and look again at the stuff you wrote down when you were dead. Look at that stuff. Those are things that you wished you could have done while you were alive. Well, YOU ARE ALIVE. So what are you going to do about those wishes?

Here's where you are going to start. Pick three things. It doesn't matter which three. Put a star by them.

Now do them! If it is something you would tell your parents, tell them. If it is letting a friend know how much you care for him, say it. If it is sending someone flowers, send them. **Whatever your three things are, do them.**

Here's the deal. We wait 'til people die to tell them how much we love them. Like sending flowers to funerals. Not too many dead people care about what kind of arrangement you sent them. When my grandmother died, I decided that I would never have to send flowers to a funeral. I was going to do it when they were alive. So now I send flowers for any reason. My favorite reason is no reason. I love sending flowers for no reason.

day 27

I wanted to let my parents know how much I loved them. It is hard for me to say that kind of stuff to the parentals so I wrote them a note. Then I made a tape with just one song on it. It talked about how as a kid the parents prayed for their kid. He grew up and didn't always make the right choices and hurt his family a lot. But he was doing OK now and just wanted to say, "Thanks for praying for me."

 I put it in an envelope and left it on the table for them to find. Not much was said about it. But I knew that my parents knew I was thankful and that I loved them.

Do and say things while you are here. Don't wait for a death so you can look at a family member and say, "John was a wonderful person." Tell John. "Hey John, you are wonderful." Don't waste the words on the dead. Give the words directly to the people. Do the things that you want to do while you're alive and they're alive.

You have 'til the end of the week to do the three things that you picked. Life is all about relationships. Make it a habit to let people know how much they mean to you. STEP OFF, and Live With No Regrets.

	PRAYER? yes		**BIBLE SURF?** yes		**NATURE?** yes

day 28

What would be the worst job you could think of having? One that you would not want. I read an article about a country that hired rat killers. No, not exterminators. Rat killers. These guys would hit the streets every night armed with sticks and kill rats. They were paid a few pennies for every dead rat they brought in. What about you? What would take the prize for worst job?

In Bible days, everyone wore sandals. Not a really great fashion statement, but shoes were still relatively new. And they had no cars so they walked everywhere. Oh yeah, and the streets were dirt. No indoor plumbing for showers or bathing. Are you starting to get the picture? Sandals, dirt, sweat, feet, no showers--there was some major foot funk going on. The job that all the servants hated was washing the guests' feet. Can you imagine? There are days that I don't even want to touch my own feet, much less someone else's. But it was a job that someone had to do.

THE WORD

Read John 13:1-17.

Jesus, God with skin, got on the ground and washed the disciples's feet. To make it even tougher, He already knew that Judas was gonna betray Him and Peter would deny he even knew Him. But still, the Leader, the Master, got down like the lowest servant and washed feet.

Whatever it takes! That was what Jesus wanted to show his followers. Whatever the need, whatever the hurt, whatever the circumstances, do whatever it takes. Money, pride, power, popularity, these things are all way down on the wish list. Top spot is serving. Helping others become more. Giving others the best seat. Finding out how to make the lives of others better and doing whatever it takes.

LIFE LINK!

Bear one anothers burdens, and so fulfill the law of Christ. (Galatians 6:2)

STEP OFF

Wash Feet.

Are you ready? You thought the Media Fast was hard. Wait 'til you try this. Your group is going to have a foot washing. This entire adventure you have been going through has been built to break down barriers and to create bonds. This will be a true test.

Get with your group members and decide the when, what, where, and all that. If you're not doing this book with a group, then call up your best friend, ask your mom, or look for someone who could use some encouragement and ask them to do this with you. Here are some guidelines to help you get started. They aren't the law. They are just to help you get in line with what we are doing.

day **28**
{continued}

SETUP

1. Decide when and where.
2. Get three or four pans, buckets, basins, whatever you are going to use to put water in.
3. Get enough washcloths and towels for everyone to have one.
4. Put warm water into the pan (cold water is a major shocker).
5. If desired, put some type of aroma salt or scented oil in the H2O (some feet may need this, plus in Bible days they used scented oils as well).
6. Choose who will start.

SYSTEM

1. Have everyone sit holding his washcloth.
2. Remove shoes and socks.
3. Starters kneel down in front of a group member.
4. Take the washcloth from the person, wet it, and wash their feet.
5. Pray for them as you are washing their feet.
6. Hand the washcloth back to the person and dry with your towel.
7. Move to the next person.
8. Wash every member's feet, praying for them as you do.
9. When you have finished, hand the water container to someone else.
10. Check the water temp. If it's getting cool, refill it.
11. Continue until everyone has washed everyone else's feet.

day 28

SCENE
1. Have the lights dimmed. (Candlelight works well too).
2. Play music in the background. (Instrumental or praise music works great).
3. Start out by having the group pray together.
4. Begin.
5. As you kneel before the person, pray for him.
6. End in prayer.

If your group comes up with some cooler stuff that will work, do it. Make it your thing. The important thing isn't to follow the directions; the important thing is that you do it!

Right now, before you go through the experience, answer these questions:

Which do you think will be harder for you?
Washing feet or having yours washed?
Why?

Having mine washed, because my feet are sickly and Embarrassing

How do you think this foot washing relates to your real life?

we all need to be cleansed. Its like hearing the word of God, it cleans us

Pray that God will show you something through this. Ask Him to help you serve others. And pray for the other people in your STEP OFF group. Ask God to prepare them for the foot washing.

You are about to push yourself into the very steps of Jesus. This is where He physically stepped out of His role as Teacher, knelt down, and became the servant. **Be bold. Stand up, kneel down, wash feet and STEP OFF.**

	PRAYER?		BIBLE SURF?
	yes		*yes*

Life is not tried
It is merely survived
If you're standing outside the fire.
--Garth Brooks, "Standing Outside the Fire"

day 29

How'd the foot washing go?

(By the way, don't do today or tomorrow until you have done the foot washing.)

You did it. You got down and did it. Give me a short description of what happened. Write it down.

Well, I came late and was tricked by everyone at the foot washing Party. They told me I had to was everyone's feet; so I did. I had a lot of fun. The others only had to wash one other persons foot.

day · · · 29

How did you feel going into it? Were you nervous, scared, excited?

I was scared about people washing my feet.

Turn back a page or two and read the answers you wrote to the questions:

"Which do you think will be harder for you?"

"How do you think this foot washing relates to your real life?"

How did you feel about washing other people's feet?

I was a little grossed out at first, but after a while, I started to enjoy it.

day 29

What did you think about getting your feet washed?

I liked it; it felt good

Which was harder?
Why?

Getting my feet washed. I didn't want people to see my feet

Now, after doing it, how do you think this relates to your real life?

We all need to have the dirt in our lives cleansed away. only Jesus can do that.

day 29

How does it connect to the LIFE LINK! verse Galatians 6:2,
"Bear one another's burdens, and so fulfill the law of Christ"?

we are being servants like Christ was

You have now experienced a tiny part in the life of a true leader, 'cause a real leader serves those around him. As the team captain, head cheerleader, class prez, you have to serve if you are going to lead. A true leader's attitude is "Whatever it takes!"

144

day · 29

Everyday we pass opportunities to serve. We miss a lot of them because we're not looking. Well look! No matter how small or how large, look for ways to help. Search for ways to wash feet and serve.

> **Don't forget about serving like the true Master.** **Remember, Jesus washed the feet of Judas and Peter even though He knew they were going to hurt Him deeply. There are people you really don't like. They may stab you in the back or say things to hurt you, but you are called to serve them too. We have been set apart to become more like Christ and serve Him by serving others.**

These are life issues. Take what we've discussed and make it happen. Serve others with all that you have. Whatever it takes...STEP OFF.

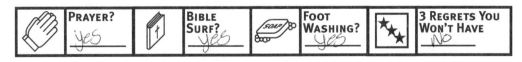

	PRAYER? yes		BIBLE SURF? yes		FOOT WASHING? yes		3 REGRETS YOU WON'T HAVE no

day 30

You made it! Let the party begin!

(Yes, I mean it. I would have a party. But hey, that's just me.)

You did it. You didn't quit. Did you want to?

Sometimes, yes

Did you want to bounce and say forget it?

Yeah, but then I'd think about
my commitment that I made

{
* Giving away something that was precious to you.
* 21 Day Media Fast.
* Committed to not ever letting there be a hint of sexual immorality.
* Where's your symbol?
* Got away with God for 1/2 a day. Just you and Him.
* Left the Christian Ghetto to come be Salty.
* You checked your friends and maybe changed who you were hanging with.

Any of these alone is tough. But you went at 'em all at one time.
You are the few. You are the survivors. You are the ones God has
called to win the battle. The battle for your friends. The battle at
school. The battle with the world, between Heaven and Hell.

FOR YOU:

What was the thing you remember most about STEP OFF?

The media fast and giving something away

What do you think you learned the most?

Committment is easier said than done.

What was the hardest part for you?

No video games for 21 days

What are some things that you learned?

If you depend on God instead of things like television, life is a lot more fun

Do you know more about what God wants? Like what?

Yes. God wants us to be examples, but we don't have to be boring

What LIFE LINK! verse helped you the most?

Romans 8:28

What is one thing that you have changed or has changed about you?

I'm not so dependent on TV. & video games

Who are some friends that you wish could go through STEP OFF?

carrie Voight, tyler Cornish Ryan marcy

As you have gone through STEP OFF, you have looked a lot at deep issues inside you and inside your friends. If you were going to put it all together and come up with the three biggest words in the world, what would they be? The three most powerful words? **Say them out loud.**

I don't know what they are.

Most people say, "I love you." Close, but no Teddy Bear. The three words that make hearts soar and move people into action are, "I need you." We all want to be needed. We have a purpose. We have a reason for being. Someone else needs us.

Well, you are needed. I need you. Your friends need you. God needs you. We all need to take the final challenge. We need you to take another group through STEP OFF. Your friends can't because they've never done it before. God could have made little clones to come down and teach it, but He's hasn't. He made you. Pick up the ball and start running.

Remember your **LIFE LINK!** verse:
Go therefore and make disciples of all the nations, baptizing them
in the name of the Father and of the Son and of the Holy Spirit.
(Matthew 28:19)

How?

* Pal up with someone in your group. The two of you take others through the adventure guide of Step Off.
* Make sure you have only two leaders.
(You don't want more leaders than groupers.)
* Start thinking about who you want in the group.

Who?

* Pray alone and with your co-leader that God will show you who to get in the group.
* You can start with others in your youth group at church, but reach outside of it. Reach out to those who are out there on the wacked-out edge. The geeks, the skaters, anyone. Take them through Step Off.

When?

* You as co-leaders decide when you will do it. What day, time, etc.
* Or you can get the group together first and then have the group decide. (Warning: It is so much easier to decide the date first, then if someone can't make it on that day, tell them that they can get in another group, or wait 'til you start another one.)

Where?

* Again, you decide.
* Make it a place where you guys can talk without interruption. (It's hard to talk with a little brother crawling all over you or with someone shouting, "Who had the vanilla latte with cream?")

What?

* Step Off
* Bible
* Trade phone numbers, e-mails, and addresses so that you can send stuff or contact each other.

WHY?

* Why You? You have been there before. You know what is going to happen. You can help lead them, so they can get the most out of Step Off.

* You can push them past where you went. You can go bigger. If you want to give away more stuff as a group, do it. If you want to extend the Media Fast, do it. Try new things to help the group step off.

* You have gone through Step Off. You should be psyched because you made it through some serious tough stuff. But, if you don't keep moving you will flat-line. You will stop growing. To get back in the groove in becoming Christ-like is you must now take others where you have been. You will probably get more out of Step Off as a leader than you did the first round.

This is the most important commitment ever in Step Off. If you stop here then the force that you've started doesn't move on. A spark ignited an explosion. But if you don't get another group going, that is like throwing water on the fire. Don't let it stop with you. Make a difference. You are needed. You are about to change lives. It's not because you can do anything. But because God can do awesome things through you, His kid, when you are willing to be used.

You have the power to say yes or no. This is the last day, so I can't tell you to get out if you don't want to do this. What I am telling you is, "GET IN!" This is the last day, but it can be the first day. Remember, it's not about you anymore. It's all about God and how He has called you to take Him to others.

1. Accept the Challenge
2. Pray. Pray. Pray. Pray that God will help you.
3. Make a Plan.
4. Don't wait. Start today.
5. Follow through.
6. STEP OFF.

PRAYER? _yes_   BIBLE SURF? _yes_   LEAD? ____

Check it out! Get involved!
Make a difference!

COMPASSION INTERNATIONAL
God can use you to change the life of a child forever.
www.ci.org

HABITAT FOR HUMANITY INTERNATIONAL
A Christian organization and welcomes volunteers from all faiths who are
committed to Habitat's goal of eliminating poverty housing.
www.habitat.org

WORLD VISION
For kids in need around the world, hope changes everything.
www.worldvision.org

NATIONAL CENTER FOR FAMILY LITERACY
Promoting family literacy services across the United States.
www.famlit.org

BIG BROTHERS BIG SISTERS OF AMERICA
Making a big difference. One child at a time.
www.bbbsa.org

AMERICARES
Bringing help and hope.
www.americares.org

VOLUNTEERMATCH.ORG
Thousands of volunteer opportunities on-line.
www.volunteermatch.org

Check out These Other Groovy Products from Extreme for Jesus

BIBLES

The Extreme Teen Bible—Hardcover	$24.99
The Extreme Teen Bible—Paperback	$19.99
The Extreme Teen Bible—Black Bonded Leather	$39.99
The Extreme Teen Bible—Deep Purple Bonded Leather	$39.99
The Extreme Teen Bible—Slimey Limey Green Bonded Leather	$39.99
The Extreme Teen Bible—Lava Orange Bonded Leather	$39.99
Extreme Word GenX Bible—Paperback	$19.99
Extreme Word GenX Bible—Chromium Hardcover	$29.99
Extreme Word GenX Bible—Blue Snake Hardcover	$29.99
Extreme Word GenX Bible—Black Vinyl	$39.99
The Extreme Teen Bible NCV—Paperback	$19.99
The Extreme Teen Bible NCV—Hardcover	$24.99
The Gospel of John	$1.50

REFERENCE BOOKS

Extreme A-Z: Find it in the Bible	$19.99
Extreme Answers to Extreme Questions	$12.99
Extreme Journey	$14.99
The Dictionary	$19.99

BOOKS

Burn—A Call to Extreme Compassion	$9.99
Genuine, by Stacie Orrico (with CD)	$13.99
Extreme Faith	$10.99

DEVOTIONALS

Extreme Encounters	$9.99

JOURNALS

Xt4J Plastic Cover Journal	$9.99
Extreme Journal	$9.99

PROMISE BOOKS

God's Promises Rock (Your World)	$3.99
Extreme Promise Book	$13.99

CALENDARS

No Repeat Days	$9.99